THE LAITY AND CHRISTIAN EDUCATION

Apostolicam Actuositatem, Gravissimum Educationis

REDISCOVERING VATICAN II

Series Editor: Christopher M. Bellitto, Ph.D.

Rediscovering Vatican II is an eight-book series in commemoration of the fortieth anniversary of Vatican II. These books place the council in dialogue with today's church and are not just historical expositions. They answer the question: What do today's Catholics need to know?

This series will appeal to readers who have heard much about Vatican II, but who have never sat down to understand certain aspects of the council. Its main objectives are to educate people as to the origins and developments of Vatican II's key documents as well as to introduce them to the documents' major points; to review how the church (at large and in its many parts) since the council's conclusion has accepted and/or rejected and/or revised the documents' points in practical terms; and to take stock of the council's reforms and paradigm shifts, as well as of the directions that the church appears to be heading.

The completed series will comprise these titles:

Ecumenism and Interreligious Dialogue: Unitatis Redintegratio, Nostra Aetate by Cardinal Edward Cassidy

The Church and the World: Gaudium et Spes, Inter Mirifica by Norman Tanner

The Laity and Christian Education: Apostolicam Actuositatem, Gravissimum Educationis by Dolores Leckey

Liturgy: Sacrosanctum Concilium by Rita Ferrone

Scripture: Dei Verbum by Ronald Witherup

The Nature of the Church: Lumen Gentium, Christus Dominus, Orientalium Ecclesiarum by Richard Gaillardetz

Evangelization and Religious Freedom: Ad Gentes, Dignitatis Humanae by Jeffrey Gros and Stephen Bevans

Religious Life and Priesthood: Perfectae Caritatis, Optatam Totius, Presbyterorum Ordinis by Maryanne Confoy

THE LAITY AND CHRISTIAN EDUCATION

Apostolicam Actuositatem
Gravissimum Educationis

Dolores R. Leckey

Paulist Press
New York/Mahwah, NJ

Cover design by Amy King

Book design by Celine M. Allen

Copyright © 2006 by Dolores R. Leckey

Library of Congress Cataloging-in-Publication Data

Leckey, Dolores R.
    The laity and Christian education : apostolicam actuositatem, gravissimum educationis / Dolores R. Leckey.
        p. cm. — (Rediscovering Vatican II)
    Includes bibliographical references and index.
    ISBN 0-8091-4220-1 (alk. paper)
    1. Vatican Council (2nd : 1962–1965). Decretum de apostolatu laicorum. 2. Christian education of adults. 3. Christian education—Philosophy. 4. Catholic Church—Education. I. Title.
    BX8301962.A45 A7435 2006
    262'.152—dc22

                                                                                        2006018120

Published by Paulist Press
997 Macarthur Boulevard
Mahwah, New Jersey 07430

www.paulistpress.com

Printed and bound in the
United States of America

Dedicated to Bishop Albert H. Ottenweller
Chairman of the National Conference of Catholic Bishops'
Committee on the Laity (1978–1981)
who has dedicated his life and ministry
to making Vatican II live
in the hearts, minds, and actions of the People of God.
And as always, for TPL

CONTENTS

Acknowledgments ix

Abbreviations xi

Preface xiii

DECREE ON THE APOSTOLATE OF THE LAITY
DECLARATION ON CHRISTIAN EDUCATION
Apostolicam Actuositatem / Gravissimum Educationis

Part I: The Documents 1

Part II: Major Points 22

Part III: Implementation 37

Part IV: The State of the Questions 86

NOTES 97

Part V: Further Reading 103

INDEX 109

ACKNOWLEDGMENTS

A number of people contributed to the making of this book. Paulist Press deserves first mention for conceiving of the series, Rediscovering Vatican II. Everyone with whom I've consulted believes the series is needed and the "discoveries" will rekindle the embers of hope and energy.

Several years ago, the Louisville Institute for Church Leadership awarded me a grant for research into Catholic Church leadership in the last quarter of the twentieth century. That project resulted in a number of articles and talks, but most important, interviews with leaders, many of them bishops, which provided primary source material for Part Three.

In 2004 I spent a month at Saint Mary's College, Notre Dame, as a Madeleva writer in residence. There I did the research for Parts One and Two and enjoyed the resources of Saint Mary's library and the library at the University of Notre Dame. I'm especially grateful to Kathleen Dolphin BVM, director of the Center for Spirituality at Saint Mary's, who hosted me for this residency, and who is herself dedicated to rekindling the spirit of the council. Roseanne Schultz, CSC, vice president for mission at Saint Mary's, went the extra mile to welcome me to that special community.

To my colleagues at the Woodstock Theological Center, I offer my gratitude for their quiet support, their willingness to critique, and their insightfulness about the importance of historical consciousness. They love to question, as befits true companions of Jesus.

My children who constantly asked, "How's the book coming?" were loving prods along the way. The editor of this series, Christopher Bellitto, also prodded, and in addition offered concrete suggestions, all of which were valuable in shaping the text. His active patience is something to emulate.

Marie Powell of the USCCB Department of Education generously shared with me official resources for the implementation of the
Decree on Christian Education; and Maria Ferrara once again provided much needed technical assistance.

Finally, the laymen and laywomen who during these last forty
years have never lost hope that the Lord is with us, and who daily act
on that hope, are on every page. Their lives praise God and enliven
the teachings of the council.

Dolores R. Leckey
The Woodstock Theological Center
December 2005

ABBREVIATIONS

Documents of Vatican II

AA	*Apostolicam Actuositatem* (Apostolate of the Laity)
AG	*Ad Gentes* (Missionary Activity)
CD	*Christus Dominus* (Bishops)
DH	*Dignitatis Humanae* (Religious Freedom)
DV	*Dei Verbum* (Revelation)
GE	*Gravissimum Educationis* (Christian Education)
GS	*Gaudium et Spes* (The Church in the World of Today)
IM	*Inter Mirifica* (Means of Social Communication/Mass Media)
LG	*Lumen Gentium* (The Church)
NA	*Nostra Aetate* (Non-Christian Religions)
OE	*Orientalium Ecclesiarum* (Eastern Catholic Churches)
OT	*Optatam Totius* (Priestly Formation)
PC	*Perfectae Caritatis* (Religious Life)
PO	*Presbyterorum Ordinis* (Ministry and Life of Priests)
SC	*Sacrosanctum Concilium* (Liturgy)
UR	*Unitatis Redintegratio* (Ecumenism)

Other Abbreviations

CCHD	Catholic Campaign for Human Development
CFM	Christian Family Movement
CL	*Christifideles Laici* (apostolic exhortation on The Christian Lay Faithful)
CTA	Call To Action
CUF	Catholics United for the Faith
ERA	Equal Rights Amendment
FADICA	Founders and Donors Interested in Catholic Activities

NAC   National Advisory Council

NCCB   National Conference of Catholic Bishops

NCCL   National Council of Catholic Laity

USCC   United States Catholic Conference

USCCB   United States Conference of Catholic Bishops

WOC   Women's Ordination Conference

YCS   Young Christian Students

YCW   Young Christian Workers

PREFACE

Paulist Press made a wise choice in joining *Apostolicam Actuositatem* (the Decree on the Apostolate of the Laity) and *Gravissimum Educationis* (the Declaration on Christian Education) in this one volume. They are natural partners. *Apostolicam Actuositatem* understands education to be a prime site for lay activity and leadership both in Catholic arenas and in secular ones. It lays out the scope and principles that are important for the lay apostolate, while *Gravissimum Educationis* illustrates how lay leadership can and should be enacted in one particular arena.

Because of their closeness, I have presented *Apostolicam Actuositatem* and *Gravissimum Educationis* together in all parts of the book. In some cases the documents are cross-referenced to show how the same or similar points appear in both.

Part Three focuses on implementation of conciliar teaching on the laity and on education as it has unfolded in the United States. There are several reasons for taking this approach. The primary one is that the United States is what I know. It's where I've spent my time and energy for a quarter of a century engaged with these documents, especially *Apostolicam Actuositatem*. The European experience has been similar to ours, except that the United States has maintained a level of religiosity not seen in Europe today. The South American, African, and Asian experiences of implementation seem best related by those "on the ground" in those places.

A word about what has been left out. Even though youth has been and continues to be a major concern of the Pontifical Council on the Laity and of the related office in the USCCB, I have not written about it in this book. Here's why. The most far-reaching program of, by, and for youth has been and is World Youth Day. These gatherings of young people from all over the world to meet with the pope are well known. Any one of these regularly scheduled events could warrant a book dedicated only to this subject. Indeed, such books and reports are available from the USCCB.

As suggested in Part Four, the current situation almost demands that laity be well informed about conciliar and papal teaching concerning their irreplaceable role in the church, as well as with the body of pastoral teaching produced by the American bishops. Hopefully this series, and in particular this volume, will help achieve that goal.

PART I

THE DOCUMENTS

BACKGROUND

The Second Vatican Council is often referred to as "The Council of the Laity." The nomenclature may be wry hyperbole, but it also contains a nugget of truth. The calling of the council by Pope John XXIII, an elderly pope expected to be simply a caretaker after the tumultuous reign of Pope Pius XII, was one of the great church surprises of the twentieth century. The fact that the council approved a decree on the laity, *Apostolicam Actuositatem* (and that lay concerns were central to many of the discussions surrounding the writing and approving of the other documents) was also surprising.

The dictum of Pope Pius X that "the one duty of the laity is to allow themselves to be led and, like a docile flock, to follow their pastors"[1] had set the tone for the laity's role in the church for generations. But for decades prior to the 1960s, the ground had been cultivated to allow for a different view of the laity's role to emerge. The currents of creative theological reflection and the unfolding of historical understanding and cultural change were being felt within the walls of the institutional church. Catholic Christian self-understanding was getting deeper and more inclusive, and European theologians and apostolic lay movements were central players in all this.

In the Forefront

French Dominicans and Jesuits were particularly influential as they worked to shape a new theology. It was a theology that was heavily dependent on biblical research while at the same time exploring the values present in the modern world. The new theologians utilized culture as a context for reflection about God and the things of God. They did not abandon Thomism (the philosophical underpinning of Catholic theology, based on the teaching of St. Thomas Aquinas, which had perdured for centuries), but rather understood it in the light of historical and cultural realities. The contemporary American theologian Paul Lakeland states that no one influenced the Second Vatican Council more than these theologians, and chief among them was Yves-Marie Congar, OP.[2]

Yves Congar, OP

In 1981, I attended a meeting in Vienna sponsored by the Pontifical Council on the Laity. Participants were European bishops who had major responsibilities for the development of the laity's role in the church. Each bishop had a lay adviser, so participants were about evenly divided between bishops and laity. Bishop Albert Ottenweller, who was then chairman of the U.S. Bishops' Committee on the Laity, was invited as an observer, and I went as his adviser.

The Vatican had invited a special guest, the esteemed Dominican theologian Père Yves Congar, who was seventy-eight years old at the time and somewhat infirm. He spoke from a wheelchair in French, his voice strong and clear, his face transparent. We knew, of course, that he was one of the architects of *Lumen Gentium* (the Dogmatic Constitution on the Church) and *Gaudium et Spes* (the Pastoral Constitution on the Church in the Modern World) and had been influential in the drafting of the Decree on the Apostolate of the Laity. That history was certainly impressive. But more than that, we sensed we were in the presence of a true believer, an authentic Christian, one who had known much suffering, and much hope.

Having been imprisoned by the Germans during World War II, he knew the hardships of war. He had also experienced the pain that the church had caused in his life. How did that happen? In the early 1950s, after the publication of two of his greatest books, *True and False Reform in the Church* and *Lay People in the Church*, Congar was silenced by the Vatican. Essentially that meant that he could neither write nor teach theology. It is thought that the Vatican's objection to these works was that they questioned the church's authority, surely a misreading. His master work, *Lay People in the Church* remains a classic regarding the theology of the laity, although in later years he feared that he, too, had fallen into the trap of defining the laity solely in relation to the clergy.[3]

A major thesis of Congar is that the laity love and serve God by their life in the world. But that is not all. The layperson also has a role in the worshiping community, bringing the things of the world, "the work of our hands," to the celebration of the Eucharist. Perhaps most important in terms of council documents and postconciliar life is Congar's probing of the power of baptism as the primary sacrament of evangelization and mission. It is this insight that has guided the life of the laity, theologically and pastorally, in the forty years since the close of the council. Once initiated into the Catholic community of faith, all are called to a life of mission—not exactly the same mission, but to lives of service and witness according to individual gifts and the needs of the community. Congar's was a strong and creative voice in the years prior to the council, full of conviction that the laity were indispensable to the mission of the church. His insight that the laity truly participate in the priesthood of Christ can be found throughout the documents of the council.

Who brought him from "church exile" into the heart of the Second Vatican Council? Pope John XXIII himself. When the new pope announced his intention to convene an ecumenical council, he also announced the formation of a preparatory commission. An event of the magnitude of the proposed council required the best theological minds of the time to lay out the parameters of the enormous task before the bishops of the world. Yves Congar, an original but careful theologian, was summoned by the pope to serve on that commission. It was a key position.

Lay Movements

While theologians like Congar were engaged in explicit theological formulations, the emerging lay movements were applying the new theology to the needs of society. The Belgian priest Father Joseph Cardign had designed a method for addressing the problems of the world. It was a method beautiful in its simplicity, and it appealed to the idealism of youth. Groups from different walks of life were formed in the method—*observe, judge, and act*—not unlike the theological imperatives of Bernard Lonergan, SJ.[4] The main groups were: (1) Young Christian Students (YCS), who applied the method to university life; (2) Young Christian Workers (YCW), who concentrated on the workplace; and (3) the Christian Family Movement (CFM), which examined familial and civic life.

Another movement, The Grail, an international lay movement for women, focused on the arts and education. When I was a college student in Brooklyn there was a Grail House nearby where several women lived together in community, their apostolate being hospitality and catechesis of the local children. Some of my friends and I helped with the instruction of the children, who were mostly from Puerto Rico. One evening we appeared at the Grail House thinking that was the evening we were invited for dinner. It was not. But the women of the Grail received us in the spirit of St. Benedict: "Receive all as Christ." Smiling, they cut their few pork chops into strips, poured half glasses of ginger ale, and created a fruit salad from an orange, a banana, and a pear. It was a memorably gracious meal.

There were other movements, most of them dedicated to helping the poor through presence and advocacy. The Catholic Worker Movement in the United States was and remains a prime example. One of the founders, Dorothy Day, situated her activism squarely in the demands of the gospel and the foundational teachings of Catholic social thought. She picketed on behalf of unions and engaged in anti-nuclear demonstrations during the Cold War period. She pressed the church she joined as an adult to be a witness to radical peace. And all the time, she never wavered from her understanding of living the Beatitudes: feeding the hungry, clothing the naked, and providing shelter for the Bowery alcoholics. She took seriously the theology of St. Thérèse of Lisieux's "little way," that is, to do small acts of mercy with love and humility. A cup of water in the name of Jesus offered to one in need reflects that "little way," as do the Catholic Worker soup kitchens.

In Europe, many of these lay activities existed under the rubric of Catholic Action, although in truth that was a distinct movement with a defined, politically framed purpose. The Catholic Action movement was to act in the world on the church's behalf, following the leadership of the hierarchy, and was most visible in Italy. Often, however, the lay apostolate associated with many of the other lay movements was also called Catholic Action. In both its senses, though, the term contained the clear understanding that the laity participated in the apostolate of the hierarchy. A distinct lay apostolate had not yet been clearly articulated, and it was this somewhat confused idea of the apostolate that most bishops brought to Vatican II.[5]

Debates about the precision of these terms occurred during the council deliberations and during the subsequent Synod on the Vocation and Mission of the Laity in the Church and in the World (1987). Linguistic sparring aside, the rise of the lay movements, the lay apostolate, brought energy to the years preceding the council, and in a way tested the relevance of the new theology for the modern world. Individual commitment was key and one exemplar of these lay movements was Rosemary Goldie whose life unfolded into several movements, including Pax Romana and The Grail.

Rosemary Goldie: Witness to Lay Empowerment

In the summer of 1936, a young Australian woman, Rosemary Goldie, sailed from Sydney, Australia, for France. She had received the French Government Traveling Scholarship, which provided for two years of study at the Sorbonne. During her brief time in France, she immersed herself in French literature and also in Catholic Action. In France, Catholic Action, influenced by Father Cardign, meant an apostolate of "like-to-like" in order to change various milieus. Goldie soon became a member of the international movement of Catholic university students called Pax Romana, which held its sixteenth congress in Paris in 1937. Pax Romana became like a family to her. She says of these years in Paris, brief though they were, "Paris was my entry into international living."[6] As Europe moved to the brink of chaos and war, Goldie made the decision to return to Australia. There she was instrumental in establishing the Pax Romana in Australia.

During the first years of the Second World War, she taught French in a Catholic college in Australia. Eventually, she joined The Grail, which she described as offering the possibility of a dedicated life for women "in the world." In fact, the major source of formation in Goldie's life became The Grail, and she exercised her mission largely in the environment of Sydney University, becoming responsible for university Grail groups. At the same time, she continued to hope that somehow she would be able to complete her doctoral thesis in French literature at the Sorbonne.

In 1945, with the war in its final months, her hope was realized. She learned that she had been awarded an international fellowship, and she prepared to return to France. While the European phase of the war was over, Japan was still engaged, and travel had many dangers. Nonetheless, Goldie took the journey to England where she waited for the right moment to return to the Sorbonne. That moment came in October 1945. Wartime conditions still prevailed in Paris, but Pax Romana was thriving, and she became focused on that organization rather than the Sorbonne. In her memoir she notes that, in the end, she never completed her thesis, although much of her research has been published in other forms. The truth is that the lay apostolate had captured her imagination and her energy.

The year 1950 was a Holy Year, and part of the celebration of that jubilee event was preparation for the First World Congress for the Lay Apostolate to be held in October 1951. All the major lay movements would participate, and Goldie was officially to be a delegate of Pax Romana, something she looked forward to with eager anticipation. The organizers of the congress had another idea though. She was asked to work in the secretariat, behind the scenes, in order to provide the needed support for this monumental gathering. Goldie's organizational abilities were needed, and she put her own desires aside for the good of the lay movements.

Pope Pius XII, who had called for the congress, had earlier (in 1946) declared that "the laity are also the church."[7] This may not seem like a revolutionary statement in the light of developments since the Second Vatican Council, but in 1951 the memory of that statement stirred hope in the hearts and spirits of the laity throughout the world. Goldie would do whatever was needed.

The First World Congress for the Lay Apostolate

Rosemary Goldie refers to this congress as "providential," and it was, insofar as it laid a foundation for all that was to follow, right up to the Second Vatican Council. The congress opened on October 7, 1951, approximately eleven years before the opening of the council. National delegations from seventy-four countries, representatives of thirty-eight Catholic international organizations, and members of seventeen ethnic groups in exile from Communist states gathered to make history. It was truly a world church congress, although, as one of the leaders sagely pointed out, it was limited to study, not legislation. Workshops were the venue for the study, with topics like parish, family, women, and work on the agenda. Notably absent was the topic of ecumenism. It would take a few more years for that to rise to the surface.

Two major speeches on "The Doctrines of the Lay Apostolate" had little in common, according to Goldie who was, of course, present for the proceedings. Valerian Gracias, archbishop of Bombay, quoted not only recent popes (a pattern in Roman meetings to this day) but also Cardinal Newman and Cardinal Suhard, both of whom had pioneered a theology of the laity that stressed shared responsibility for the church's mission. He also invoked two English laymen, G. K. Chesterton, a writer and convert to Catholicism, and Frank Sheed, who along with his wife Maisie Ward founded the Sheed & Ward Publishing Company.

The other speaker, an Argentine cardinal, Antonio Caggianno, emphasized the subordination of the lay apostolate to the hierarchy. These divergent positions would later be heard in the council debates.

One of the outstanding presentations was given by an American laywoman, Catherine Schaeffer, who served as liaison for the American bishops with the United Nations. "The United Nations has now been in existence for six precarious years," she said. "It is responsible for the maintenance of peace in the whole world . . . a world made small by the tremendous strides of technical progress, and united in fear of the great destruction which that progress has made possible."[8] These words have a poignant relevance for our own time, and still give pause about the laity's role as members of an international church.

The congress itself lasted only a week, but it gave birth to a vital entity for the empowerment of the laity. The first was the establishment of a Permanent Committee, the basic structure of which was an office in Rome, which prepared for future congresses and which kept in touch with various international organizations. One feature of this new, though small, secretariat was the influential role played by women who quietly undertook the tasks of leadership.

Discussions continued about exactly what constituted Catholic Action and what constituted the lay apostolate. Some of the committees spoke about the lay apostolate as merely a metaphor. Father Cardign dismissed that suggestion, calling the laity's leadership in the world a life-and-death matter for the church. The lines continued to be drawn around definition and, more important, theological understanding.

The Second World Congress for the Lay Apostolate

By the time the Second World Congress opened in October 1957, many of these issues had coalesced around the congress theme, "The Crisis of the Modern World: Responsibilities and Formation." Theological experts began their preparatory work months ahead. One of them, Sebastian Tromp, SJ, was to become the secretary of the Theological Commission, a key body in the preparation for the Second Vatican Council (which had not yet been announced). Father Tromp was clearly in the wing that favored church rapprochement with the modern world. Part of the rapprochement was recognition of the key role laity had on the threshold of church and world. Once again, Pope Pius XII spoke on the opening day of the congress, and he maintained the distinction between the lay apostolate and Catholic Action, seeing the latter as being primarily the action arm of the hierarchy. Meanwhile, other countries had crafted different models, less centralized and with enough elasticity for creativity and response to rapidly changing needs.

The workshops of this second congress were all devoted to formation of the laity for the apostolate. Rosemary Goldie was convinced that much could be learned from the formation method of Young Christian Students (YCS) who, she said, as adults were surely passing on the fruits of their formation to the next generation, either through parenting or through teaching. Goldie felt that Cardign himself was not convinced by her argument. Nevertheless, some years later, at the 1987 synod on the laity a young English woman, Patricia Jones, a pastoral worker in a Liverpool parish, credited her own formation in faith to the YCS when she addressed the synod. Jones also pointed out that her parents had been deeply influenced by the Young Christian Workers movement and the insights of Cardign. So, in fact, Father Cardign's movement, in its several manifestations, had been a conductor of spirituality for the laity. One could say that Rosemary Goldie's convictions about formation were vindicated during that synod.

One of the speakers at the 1957 congress was Archbishop Montini of Milan, later to become Pope Paul VI. His comments generated sustained applause when he described the genius of the apostolate as "to know how to love....We will love our times, our community, our technical skills, our art, our sport, our world....We will love with the heart of Christ."[9] These ideas of Montini would find their way, both implicitly and explicitly, into *Apostolicam Actuositatem*.

Creative activism inspired the congress to seek out "witnesses," laymen and laywomen well known and respected in different fields and from all the continents, to write pertinent articles in a volume entitled *The World Is Waiting for the Church*. An American contributor was George Meaney of the ALF-CIO, who called for a consensus to safeguard progress for the betterment of humankind.

One of the major theological themes in these years preceding the calling of the council was the need for a positive definition of the lay Christian. Some of the greatest theological minds of the period—Yves Congar, Karl Rahner, Edward Schillebeeckx—grappled with this. At the same time, theologically aware people were writing and speaking about holiness residing in lay life, stating that holiness was not exclusively reserved for monasteries or clergy. Both of these themes found a home in council documents, which highlighted a new understanding of the laity's role in the church and in the world. Some of the leading American Catholic laity—journalists, intellectuals, and activists—were raising another important point: it was time to get beyond the idea that a good Catholic layperson was characterized by unthinking obedience.

Christian Education

Meanwhile, the laity's role in the educational enterprise was undergoing change. In the United States, an extensive parochial school system had benefited from the presence of religious sisters and brothers in huge numbers. Women religious, in particular, were the heart and soul of parish schools. There was one notable problem, however. These sisters were not permitted to pursue advanced theological studies. Well-known institutions of higher education, such as The Catholic University of America, did not admit any layperson, male or female, into advanced theological studies.

The situation was first noted by the National Catholic Education Association in the 1940s, which asked Sister Madeleva Wolff, CSC, then president of Saint Mary's College in Notre Dame, Indiana, to see if some of these institutions would examine their exclusionary policies and admit women religious. The answer she received was an unambiguous "No." Sister Madeleva, stepping out in faith, then announced that Saint Mary's would offer a six-week summer course in advanced theology. In 1944, the School of Sacred Theology, with an excellent faculty, was open for business. When the School of Sacred Theology closed twenty-five years later, Saint Mary's had granted 76 doctoral and 354 master's degrees in theology to sisters, laywomen, and laymen.[10]

The Sister Formation Movement began almost simultaneously, again with initial leadership from Sister Madeleva who wrote that, "the fact of sister-shortage, sisters' education, sisters' salaries are at last coming out in the open."[11] Bringing to light these issues helped change the face of Catholic education, and influenced the council deliberations about the state of Christian education.

These two innovations, the School of Sacred Theology and the Sister Formation Movement, enhanced the status of women in the church by assuring that they could receive an education that prepared them for roles in the modern world.[12] To talk about Catholic education in the United States, then, is to talk about the changing role of women.

Not only did students in Catholic schools benefit from the expertise of women religious, themselves now immersed in higher education, so did the thousands of children who attended public schools.

These children learned the fundamentals of the Catholic faith in special religious education classes, either during "released time" in the course of the school week, or on the weekend in Sunday school. In the years before the council the religious education program was known as the Confraternity of Christian Doctrine, or CCD for short. The teachers were mostly religious, but occasionally a layperson (usually a woman) would assist.

The teaching of religion began to move beyond memorization of the catechism. New pedagogies were introduced, influenced to some extent by the work of Maria Montessori, a pioneer in the area of early childhood education. Montessori was Italian, a deeply spiritual person, who believed that children's experiences were to be respected. Her method was to engage the whole child in the educational enterprise. Teachers of religious education began to experiment with this holistic approach, and the method found a receptive hearing during the council deliberations.

In many ways, by the time the Second Vatican Council was convened in the fall of 1962, the movements and organizations that had been promoting increased responsibility for the laity within the church and those that had been exploring the new frontiers of Christian education converged in significant ways. For example, the Christian Family Movement emphasized that parents, rather than the institutions of either church or state, were the primary educators of their children. This view was shared by religious educators. Furthermore, as laity moved closer to the center of the church, so too did the sacrament of marriage, which had implications for educators. Slowly and steadily, then, in the years just prior to the council, a whole array of issues relating to education were joined with the call for the laity to share responsibility for the mission of the church.

THE COUNCIL: SOME HIGHLIGHTS

Lay Auditors

Auditors—the word is Latin in origin—were invited to the council by Pope Paul VI. Their role was to listen and to generally be a presence in the midst of the council. In 1963, thirteen men were appointed, and a year later ten women religious and thirteen laywomen received an invitation. Rosemary Goldie, interviewed shortly before the appointment of the women auditors, remarked:

> When the men were appointed as auditors, Catholic women rejoiced. They saw this as a symbolic gesture which was mainly important for the promise it gave of a more effective and more fully recognized presence of the laity in the apostolate of the Church. Inevitably, however, the women asked themselves as did lay men, priests, bishops...even cardinals, why there was no woman in this little group.[13]

The situation was remedied largely due to the influence of Cardinal Suenens, who was able to allay fears, however unreasonable they may have been. It was he who pointed out that the draft on *Lumen Gentium* was silent about one-half of humanity. Pope Paul VI announced at a Mass celebrated at Castel Gandolfo on September 8, 1964, his intention to include "qualified and dedicated women" as auditors. "These women," said the pope, "would discuss matters of particular interest to women." Goldie asks, interestingly, "What matters of Church life would *not* be of interest to women?"[14]

Another breakthrough regarding the role of the laity during the third session of the council occurred when Patrick Keegan, president of the International Catholic Workers' Movement, addressed the council during the course of one of its business sessions. It was "a first" for a modern ecumenical council. Two other laymen had spoken during the second session of the council; Jean Guitton, a French writer, and Vittorino Veronese of Italy had made presentations on a specially designated day. So Keegan's speech was, symbolically at least, a major event for lay participation, even though, in the opinion of some, the speech seemed "clericalized."[15]

The auditors, happy to have had a representative voice (whether clerical or not) in Keegan, hoped that a woman's voice would also be heard. They, in fact, proposed Pilar Bellisolo of Spain, president of the World Union of Catholic Women's Organizations as a speaker. The proposal went nowhere. The renowned British economist, Barbara

Ward, had also hoped to speak to the council about the economically undeveloped, that is, the poor of the world. That hope also fell by the wayside. Instead, a paper she had prepared was read by a male observer. But the question of women did not disappear.

Voices of Women

The women auditors believed that documents such as *Gaudium et Spes* should take a strong stand against discrimination but should avoid any attempt to define particular roles for women or describe personality traits inherent in women. This belief carried over into *Apostolicam Actuositatem*, which stated a general principle: "Since in our time women are taking an increasingly active share in the whole life of society, it is very important that their participation in the various sections of the Church's apostolate should likewise develop" (*AA*, 9). The truth, however, is that as the debate moved forward about lay participation in the church's life, everything said about laity applied to women as well as to men.

One bishop drew murmurs of assent from the women auditors when he stated that the equal dignity of men and women constituted "a sign of the times." That phrase had become a leitmotif of the council (leaders were to look for "the signs of the times"), and so it carried some weight in the *aula* (i.e., the "hall," or council chamber). The phrase became key to understanding the relationship between the church and the world, a relationship that the council ultimately described as one of dialogue. Furthermore, the church was cautioned to shape its pastoral agenda accordingly. Clearly, the role of women was slowly becoming a sign not to be missed.

Observers and *Periti*

It must be pointed out that the overall environment at the council played some part in establishing a spirit of openness, a quality necessary to produce *Apostolicam Actuositatem* as well as many of the other documents.

A major factor was the presence of official observers from other Christian churches. They represented the main non-Roman churches except for the Greek Orthodox, the World Baptist Alliance, and certain fundamentalist churches. The observers, who were welcomed at the opening session by Pope John XXIII as honored guests in the Father's house, were admitted to the daily sessions of the council and provided with translators, a necessary courtesy since the business of the council was conducted in Latin. The observers could also attend the meetings of the commissions which were the working groups charged with revising the various drafts. So, these "other Christians," with their different experiences of lay participation and leadership, were quietly able to illustrate how things might work differently. They had no vote, but they had voice and they were a respected presence.

Equally important as attendance at commission meetings were conversations around the coffee bars set up in the niches and hallways adjacent to the meeting hall. The coffee bars were frequented by the *periti* (the expert theological advisers) and there were luminaries in their number. Observers and sometimes bishops also could be found there. Over coffee, conversation began and deepened. Ideas were exchanged and common ground was cultivated. So powerful were these conversations that some of the American observers and *periti* decided to continue their dialogues of faith, resolving to meet once a year, alternating between Catholic and Protestant settings and focusing on the general topic of spirituality.

These post-council meetings commenced in the late sixties, immediately after the close of the council, before spirituality became a discrete theological category. Gradually they coalesced into what came to be known as the Ecumenical Institute of Spirituality. The founders were the eminent Quaker Douglas Steere, a professor of ethics at Haverford College and a student of mysticism who was an official observer; Father Godfrey Diekman, OSB, a Benedictine liturgist from St. John's College in Minnesota and a *peritus*; Thomas Clarke, SJ, also a *peritus*; and Father Jean LeClerc, OSB. These gifted theologians crafted a vision of the Institute and then held it together for many years. In the beginning, the members were all men, but after a little while women were invited, one or two at a time. Over the years, the group has grown to almost equal numbers of men and women, Catholic and Protestant.

Informal Dialogues

Coffee bars were not the only sites for conversation. There were also homes—one might say homes away from home, in Rome—where ideas for *aggiornamento* and hopes for the council and the church could be discussed in a climate of candor and respect. One such home was the Foyer Unitas located on the Piazza Navonne. It was there that many of the observers were housed. Foyer Unitas was cared for by the Ladies of Bethany, a Belgian order dedicated to ecumenism, a perfect residential choice for guests from other Christian churches. Bishops were frequent visitors and many interesting conversations took place there over a bowl of soup and bottle of wine.

Another "home away from home" was located in the hills high above Rome. This was a villa rented for the duration of the council by Mrs. J. Peter Grace (Margie), an American and a dedicated member of the Legion of Mary. Leading prelates availed themselves of the Grace hospitality to invite many people who had gathered on the sidelines of the council to come to the villa for an exchange of experience and hope. It became a site for sharing the different methods of lay formation for the apostolate. The American priest, Father Pelton, who had begun the Family Rosary project; Martin Work, who had long been a promoter of the lay apostolate in the United States and, indeed, in the world; and Dorothy Day of the Catholic Worker Movement were among the many "presenters" at the villa. Cardinal Suenens, who was to be a key player in shaping the final form of *Apostolicam Actuositatem*, was often present in both homes. One can only imagine the richness of the exchanges that took place in those settings.[16]

The Council's Third Session:
A Critical Juncture for *Apostolicam Actuositatem*

Midway through the third session of the Second Vatican Council, the question that had been on the minds of many bishops began to be voiced: Could the council conclude this year, 1964, or was a fourth session needed? The third session had begun with interventions (statements) from the minority of conservatives stating certain concerns (specifically about a married deaconate and about collegiality) and generally raising the anxiety level in the hall. There were efforts to sidetrack the Declaration on Religious Freedom as well as the document on non-Christian religions, *Nostra Aetate.*

Majority leaders knew they had to act, and so on Sunday evening October 11, 1964, a group met in the residence of Cardinal J. Frings of Germany. The group was comprised mostly of Europeans, but the American cardinals Albert Meyer and Joseph Ritter were also present. Cardinal Leon-Joseph Suenens, who had been spending a few days in his Belgian homeland, hurried back to Rome to participate in the meeting. The group crafted a letter to Pope Paul VI that began, *"Magno cum dolore"*—"With great sorrow." The letter stated that a minority group wanted to return key documents to a mixed committee, *not* the official Theological Commission. Furthermore, this new committee had three members unalterably opposed to the statements in question. Expressing their "extreme anxiety" about this course of events, the group asked the pope to insist that *Dignitatis Humanae* be returned to the normal procedures of the council. They added, "To do otherwise would be extremely prejudicial to the whole Church in the light of world opinion."[17]

The pope assured Cardinal Frings that the documents in question would remain under the jurisdiction of the proper commission, but the Declaration on Religious Freedom would be "examined" by a committee formed according to council rules. Added to this mix of unfinished business was *Apostolicam Actuositatem*, which would surely be affected by the fate of the documents mentioned.

Still, council fathers were divided on whether to support a fourth session. English bishops were in favor of a fourth session, but the Canadians wanted to end the council in 1964. The Americans fell on either side of the question. Cardinal Krol wanted to conclude, while Cardinal Meyer worked hard to achieve consensus for a fourth session. Cardinal Doepfner of Germany proposed reducing many of the schemata to a series of propositions. That plan was rejected and "tilted the scales in favor of prolongation of the Council, thus saving certain highly important documents from oblivion."[18]

The debate on the draft for *Apostolicam Actuositatem*, while vividly illustrating how much work was needed on that document, also made clear that the council wanted a separate and whole document on the lay apostolate, not a list of propositions and not an appendix to another document. For five days in October 1964 the draft was debated and, according to Xavier Rynne, the debate not only marked a decision to produce a full text but also was a turning point in the exchanges and the tone of the council.[19] For the first time, attention was given by the church to the corporate function of the laity as an integral part of the People of God.

The draft was presented by Cardinal Cento, chairman of the Conciliar Commission on the Apostolate of the Laity, who, again according to Rynne,[20] apparently assumed it would be received benevolently and easily accepted. Not so. One speaker after another condemned the draft. Most of the criticism centered around two defects: (1) no layperson had been consulted until the eleventh hour, and since the document was about the lay apostolate, the bishops thought such neglect unconscionable; and (2) the material was badly arranged. For example, the theological foundation for explicating the essential role of the laity (namely the power of baptism) that appeared in *Lumen Gentium* did not reappear in *Apostolicam Actuositatem*. Also, a section on lay activity in the world, which could be found in the draft of *Gaudium et Spes*, was omitted from *Apostolicam Actuositatem*. Such omissions were not acceptable to a large majority of bishops, Bishop De Roo of Canada said. *Apostolicam Actuositatem* thus "sidestepped any real discussion of the laity's character or the spirit of their vocation."[21]

Cardinal Ritter said the draft suffered from three main defects: "clericalism, juridicism, and favoritism." By favoritism, he meant that it tended to favor Catholic Action too much at the expense of other forms of Catholic lay activity. The clericalism charge was echoed by others. "Clericalism is the enemy," said a prelate from Northern Rhodesia, "the number one enemy!" Bishop Carter of Canada went further, charging that the schema was "conceived in the sin of clericalism." He noted that by the time the laity were invited to take part in preparing the schema, it was already too late. The Dutch warned against giving the impression that what the church really wanted was to build a "clericalist civilization."

Obviously not everyone was in agreement with the notion of clericalism being a sin. A Spanish bishop professed himself "shocked" by allegations on the floor that the text was too clerical. Rynne, commenting on the Spanish intervention, opined that the bishop's solution was to banish all such thoughts by considering that ultimately everybody, including the laity, was subject to the pope and "without the pope" there is no apostolate. He then proceeded to embark on a diatribe about religious liberty, denouncing it as a "liberty to sin." He was called to order by the moderator but had difficulty getting back on track. Such denunciations were rare, though.[22]

In a lengthy and far-ranging intervention, the Indian archbishop D'Souza's candor was startling and refreshing. It was time, he said, to start considering the laity as grown-ups. He warned his confreres not to abuse the principle stated centuries ago by St. Ignatius of Antioch, a principle quoted in the draft: "Let nothing be done without the bishop." He argued that nothing should be done *against* the bishop, but much could be done without his immediate cooperation. He then turned his attention to freedom. "The People of God [a phrase that had become familiar to the bishops from *Lumen Gentium*] are not a totalitarian state." He objected particularly to the "totalitarian" implications of Catholic Action as practiced in certain Latin American countries where no other outside activities by the laity were countenanced unless they could be proven to fit with Catholic Action. He then turned to collaboration. "Laymen must be treated as brothers by the clergy and the latter must no longer attempt to usurp responsibilities which properly belong to the former." He continued, "Why could they not represent the Church in international organizations, Roman congregations, and serve in the diplomatic service of the Holy See?"[23]

The assembled council members may have been startled by the archbishop's concrete examples, but years later, at the 1987 synod on the laity, when the American bishops made an intervention on the role of women in the church, they argued in a vein similar to that of the Indian archbishop. They asked that women be allowed to represent the church according to their competence where ordination is not required, and they pointed out there are many such situations. They specifically cited the Holy See's diplomatic service as an example of what is possible.[24]

D'Souza's comments about Catholic Action elicited varied responses from council members. In 1964 the term was favored in Latin countries and in France, but less so among German Catholics, and there was basically no enthusiasm for it in English-speaking countries. Trying to steer a middle course about this contentious term the schema seemed to please neither side. Cardinal Suenens proposed some structured inquiry in order to arrive at a better definition of the term. The Second World Congress for the Lay Apostolate (1957) had been helpful in this matter and Suenens, citing the congress, offered this: Catholic Action is a *genus*, not a specific form of activity. He used the Legion of Mary as an example. The Legion was an early form of evangelization founded by an Irish layman, Frank Duff, which the Belgian cardinal supported in many ways.[25] As stated earlier, the main objection to the generally accepted criteria of Catholic Action was the perception of dominance by the hierarchy. The Legion of Mary, on the other hand, was a collaborative initiative of clergy *and* laity.

Cardinal Ritter offered his own outline of what he thought the document should look like. First, it should state the importance of the apostolate in the life of the church. This was really a critical point, since it brought the lay apostolate from the margins of the church to the heart of it. Second, he said that various forms of the apostolate should be distinguished, but not by their relationship to the hierarchy as in the present draft, which clearly reflected the Catholic Action model. And third, he wanted the document to deal with holiness and the spirituality of the laity. The way had been opened for this last point by *Lumen Gentium*'s recognition of the universal call to holiness, which stated that holiness is *one*, even while its forms and tasks are many (*LG*, 41).

With Ritter's plan before the assembly, and therefore the likelihood that the task would not be lost, bishops continued a candid critique and became creative in their suggestions. Bishop Lazlo of Austria illustrated the heart of the problem when he told the assembly he looked up "layman" in an old theological dictionary and found that the entry said, "see clergy." Decades later, during the 1987 Synod on the Vocation and Mission of the Laity in the Church and in the World, the issue of defining laity in negative terms still hung over the discussions. When the pope's exhortation *Christifideles Laici* (The Christian Lay Faithful) was issued a year after the synod, the intent was clear that the term "laity" should be understood as full membership in the church. "Incorporation into Christ through faith and Baptism is the source of being a Christian in the mystery of the Church" (*CL*, 9).

The council was searching for ways to share responsibility for church governance. Bishop Leven of San Antonio (Texas) suggested that every bishop should have a lay senate consisting of laity on whom he could call for advice and who could explain to him the desires and wishes of the laity. A similar idea was voiced by Archbishop Seper of Zagreb, Yugoslavia, who called for *weekly* meetings of laymen representing each parish in every diocese to discuss current problems.[26] (Note that the laity were often referred to as lay*men*, a sign of the times regarding the church in the mid-sixties.) The Seper plan would surely have been the logistical challenge of the century!

What these suggestions regarding participation point to, however, is the growing sense in the council that dialogue would be the key to renewal in the church. The prelates of the Eastern rite were in agreement and pointed out that cooperative relationships with the laity were much more of an assured thing in the East than in the West, which tended to overemphasize the juridical. The patriarchs were confident about the value of dialogue. The patriarchal vicar for Egypt, Archbishop Zoghby, described how in every town where there was a parish—he was speaking in regard to the Melkites—there existed a patriarchal commission, two-thirds of whom were elected by the people and one-third of whom were appointed by the patriarch. These commissions were engaged in all kinds of activities, he said: education, acting as a church court in disputed matters, managing church property and various gatherings. Anticipating objections from his confreres, he added that the faithful did not try to impose their will but rather offered help and advice. However, he noted that those bishops who disregarded informed advice would soon lose their authority over the faithful.

Archbishop Duval of Algiers took the issue of dialogue in a new direction. He focused not so much on internal relations as on the impact that the church could be expected to make on those outside, for example, the Muslims. Obviously, in Algiers the archbishop had experience in such matters, and he urged elasticity regarding boundaries of dialogue. (His point is clearly relevant today.) Exchange with others can be enriching for all, he pointed out. Along these same lines, a French bishop wanted a more open (and trusting) attitude toward the laity who live and work among non-believers. He noted that the ordinary daily life of the layperson constitutes the foundation upon which the gospel is built.

A number of speakers noted that the schema did not bring out clearly enough the real basis for the lay apostolate, namely, the royal priesthood of Christ in which *all* share through baptism and confirmation. The Canadians picked up on this theme.

Bishop De Roo, speaking in the name of fifteen bishops, urged a more theologically oriented preface, one that stressed the dual vocation of man [*sic*]: namely, to build the world and to build the church. He insisted that Christian concern for the world is not merely humanitarian but is also authentically religious and that, in fact, the two principles are inseparable.[27]

It was generally agreed that a secretariat was needed within the Roman curia if the decree on the lay apostolate, whatever its final form, were to be authentically implemented. Archbishop Heenan of Westminster expressed the thought of many when he said, "This Secretariat will be unique among the secretariats of the Holy See." And what would characterize its uniqueness? For one thing, the archbishop proposed that most of the members be chosen from the laity. He stressed that, in fact, the laity should be consulted about *how* this new secretariat should be set up, and how it should be run. "The proper thing for us to do," said Heenan, "is to learn from them." He was proposing not exclusion of ecclesiastics but the recognition of the competency and dedication of laymen and laywomen. He urged that the secretariat not be staffed by "old gentlemen who are loaded down with ecclesiastical honors." "Rather," he pleaded, "we must also choose some of our young men and women, who have to earn their daily bread."[28]

Stirring words aside, the draft of *Apostolicam Actuositatem* had little to say about the secretariat that everyone agreed was needed. The bishops wanted this omission remedied. Indeed, the sentiment of the council fathers toward the end of session three was that a major revision of the draft decree on the lay apostolate was in order. And, indeed, with the assurance that a fourth session of the council would be held in 1965, the council fathers departed the third session with a sense of confidence that a satisfactory decree could and would be crafted.

PART II

Major Points

THE COUNCIL: SESSION FOUR

When the fourth and final session of the council opened on September 14, 1965, the bishops had basically set the agenda for this last phase of their work. The Declaration on Religious Freedom was to be the first document presented for a vote. Other documents previously debated also awaited a vote, among them the Decree on the Apostolate of the Laity (*Apostolicam Actuositatem*) and the Declaration on Christian Education (*Gravissimum Educationis*).

One huge task of this last session was the debate on Schema 13, which would become *Gaudium et Spes*. An area of heated discussion was that of marriage and family, and especially the contentious issue of birth control. Some prelates wanted a restating of Pius XI's *Casti Connubii* while the commission working on Schema 13 did not. Moreover, on the sidelines was Pope Paul VI's personal attention to marriage and family life issues. All of these documents, in one way or another, had the potential to deeply affect the life of the laity.

THE DECLARATION ON CHRISTIAN EDUCATION

The Declaration on Christian Education (*Gravissimum Educationis*) generated mild debate. It seemed that the bishops had concluded that the best they could do with regard to education would be to forward a series of propositions to the pope, who could then prepare a proclamation. One might say that *Gravissimum Educationis* was a rare document in that agreement seemed in abundance and histrionics were minimal.

Perhaps they were saving their energy for *Gaudium et Spes* and *Dignitatis Humanae*.

Gravissimum Educationis was promulgated by Pope Paul VI on October 28, 1965. Contemporary educators recognized in the document many of their own priorities. For example, true education is said to aim at the formation of the human person which itself can contribute to the good of society. Application of advances in psychology and in the arts and science of teaching are recommended for the education of children and young people. Included in these advances, declared the council, should be "a positive and prudent sexual education" (*GE*, 1). Furthermore, young people should be trained to become actively involved in community organizations, skilled in dialogue, and ready to contribute to the common good. The council exhorted those with responsibility for education to see that youth are never deprived of their rights, and exhorted the church to actively care for the entire field of education, not only *religious* education.

Specifically regarding Christian education, the council held that, in addition to promoting full human maturity, there needs to be ongoing learning through liturgy, through the works of justice and the holiness of truth.

It unambiguously stated that parents are to be recognized "as the primary and principal educators" of their children (*GE*, 3). They are to do this in the atmosphere of a loving family, where the sacrament of matrimony empowers the parents. But this educational "call" is not to wall off the family from the community. On the contrary, it is to gradually lead to "a companionship with their fellowmen and with the People of God" (*GE*, 3). The proclamation also states that civil society, too, has rights in education, among them to see that the common good is promoted and that the rights of parents are protected.

What about the role of the church? Clearly, the document recognizes that the church has a deep and abiding interest in the educational process, particularly regarding youth. Priority should be given to catechesis, to communications and media, to youth groups, and to schools. In fact, schools are seen to have a primary role, right behind the family, in the education of youth. One important value, we read, is that schools offer a diversity that brings together students of different talents and backgrounds, thereby training students to learn the importance of friendly relations and mutual understanding. These particular points—parents as primary educators, approval of prudent sex education, the value of diversity—have a kind of prophetic quality to them when we consider the educational urgencies of the twenty-first century.

Teaching is seen as a true vocation, and teachers are urged to be ready "to renew and adapt" (*GE*, 5). The notion of parents as the primary educators of their children and the notion of schools that are formative as well as educational come together in a call for parents to enjoy "true liberty" in the choice of schools, and this liberty includes some form of public subsidy (*GE*, 6). Parent associations are encouraged in order to assist schools in their work of education, and in particular in moral education.

Recognizing that many of the faithful would not have religious schools available to them, the council believed the church had to be present in appropriate ways in non-religious schools. How? "By the witness of the lives of the teachers...and by the ministry of priests and laymen [*sic*]...who provide spiritual aid in every way the times and conditions allow" (*GE*, 7). Here we see one of the earlier mentions of what would become a postconciliar phenomenon, one that would stir much debate, namely "lay ministry." (Seeds of "lay ministry" are also sowed in *Apostolicam Actuositatem*.)

The thorny question of providing for direct religious education is addressed in the document. It is not surprising that the council reminds parents that they are to be activists in securing assistance in the Christian formation of their children. At the same time, the council recognized that some civil societies do, in fact, assist families in securing such religious education in non-religious schools under the banner of pluralism and religious freedom. In fact, *Dignitatis Humanae*, the Declaration on Religious Freedom, references this point (*DH*, 10).

The final sections of the Declaration on Christian Education are devoted to Catholic schools. These sections had special resonance in the United States, which at the time of the council had the most extensive and developed Catholic school system in the world. In the document the Catholic school is envisioned as an aid to fostering the dialogue between the church and humankind. Such a dialogue is understood as contributing to the betterment of culture. Key to the success of the Catholic schools are the teachers who must be properly prepared in both secular and religious disciplines, and who must be qualified in their fields and pedagogically skillful. Further, still recognizing parents as primary educators, the concept of partnership is urged, with teachers and parents working collaboratively.

While all Catholic schools will share a common core of values, *Gravissimum Educationis* understands that these schools may be organized in different forms. Of special concern are the schools established in the areas of the "new churches," presumably those in developing nations where students may not all be Catholic.

Primary and secondary Catholic schools have an undeniable importance in the life of the church, but the council fathers also assigned great importance to adult education and to special education. Interestingly, the growth of adult education in the years immediately following the close of the council can claim a mandate from that small section of the declaration, although in subsequent years various papal exhortations, usually the fruit of international synods, underscored the value and necessity of continuing education and formation in the faith.

Finally, the Declaration on Christian Education turned to Catholic colleges and universities. Of immense importance is the affirmation of scientific inquiry in a climate of freedom, something essential to the quality of education at that level, and for confidence in the integrity of the educational enterprise in Catholic institutions. In Catholic universities in which there were no faculties of sacred theology, the council called for the establishment of institutes of theology, with an explicit call for lectures suitable for lay students. (One is reminded here of the pioneering work of Sister Madeleva Wolffe and the School of Sacred Theology at Saint Mary's College.) In the sacred sciences, as in other disciplines, the spirit of penetrating inquiry is applauded.

The document sees cooperation as a value to be promoted in all areas of education. In particular, the council believed that universities would benefit from interdisciplinary efforts, the exchange of professors, and the promotion of international gatherings. The council's vision of Christian education was decidedly global.

The collaborative nature of religious education, with priests, laity, and religious men and women working together in common mission, is cited with gratitude and with a plea for them to "persevere generously in the work they have undertaken" (*GE*, Conclusion), not only for the renewal of the church but also for the benefit of the modern world.

THE DECREE ON THE APOSTOLATE OF THE LAITY

While bishops were fine-tuning *Apostolicam Actuositatem*, confident that it would pass during the fourth session, the expected spirited and serious debate was under way regarding *Gaudium et Spes*, which was taking on the form of a constitution, but one with the important adjective—*pastoral*. This pastoral constitution would certainly affect the life of the laity and was, in fact, complementary to *Apostolicam Actuositatem*. In *Gaudium et Spes* we find the fullest discussion of marriage and family life as pronounced by the council. For example, marriage is named a covenant and is described as a partnership (*GS*, 48). The official "marriage language" is no longer legalistic; rather, it is the language of love, with the understanding that marital love not only enriches the participants but also partakes in divine love. This recasting of marriage had particular resonance with laywomen and laymen.

Apostolicam Actuositatem does touch on marriage and family life, but not in such depth as *Gaudium et Spes*. The concern in *Apostolicam Actuositatem* is to emphasize that family life and secular concerns are, in fact, the stuff of holiness in the life of the laity (*AA*, 4).

Several themes in the Decree on the Apostolate of the Laity were particularly influential in the years following the council. The first of these themes is that of "vocation." The decree opens with an affirmation that the laity have a true vocation, that is, they are called by God to forward the reign of God in the world and in the church. It can be argued that this is "breakthrough" language. Why? Because it applies to all laity. Previously, the term "vocation" had been applied to ordained and vowed religious, although marriage was often described as a vocation. But *Apostolicam Actuositatem* goes beyond that, adding that the Holy Spirit is making the laity more conscious of their calling and their responsibility. Specifically, this vocation is to be the apostolate, where the laity share in the redemptive work of Christ, so that through the laity the whole world may enter into a relationship with Christ.

The vision of the lay vocation is that of activity rather than passivity. The apostolate is held up as the way in which the church carries on Christ's mission in various ways through all the members, since the laity share in the *priestly, prophetic, and royal office of Christ.* This is a key point, because it is the theological root for the flourishing of lay ministry in the post-council years.

The sacraments of baptism and confirmation are particularly important for understanding the laity's mission as a share in Christ's priestly, prophetic, and royal office. It can be argued that these sacraments deeply inform the theology of lay ecclesial ministry.[1]

Apostolicam Actuositatem states that while there is diversity of ministry, there is oneness of mission (*AA,* 2). Now, this is foundational: because the laity live in the world, they exercise the apostolate in the world. *Apostolicam Actuositatem* is thus in perfect alignment with *Gaudium et Spes,* refusing to set up the church and world as antagonists.

Elaborating on the theme of diversity, the decree speaks of charisms, or different gifts, which the laity have been given to "build the reign of God." Here we can see the hand of Cardinal Suenens, who did so much during the debate to ensure that the Holy Spirit would be properly recognized and that the theology of St. Paul's first letter to the Corinthians would find a place (*AA,* 3).

The word "freedom" is found in the document, and again the influence of Cardinal Suenens is evident. Freedom is used in reference to the charisms, reminding all that "the Holy Spirit breathes where he wills." While pastors have the responsibility to make judgments about the true nature and use of the laity's gifts—as a kind of system of checks and balances—implicit in this point is that laity ought to be trusted, certainly a stance one might hope will return to the church.

The word "spirituality" is mentioned in the decree, perhaps one of the first places in which it makes an appearance (*AA,* 4). Up to this time, "spirituality" was a word that had not been common in Catholic lexicons. If the topic arose at all, it was usually found in moral theology writings. Forty years ago there were not whole sections of bookstores dedicated to writings on the spiritual life as we find today. But *Apostolicam Actuositatem*—no doubt inspired by *Lumen Gentium*—which had been issued in an earlier session—emphasizes that the laity's life in the spirit occurs in the very web of their existence (see

LG, 30). Their spiritual life "should take its particular character from their married or family state or their single or widowed state, from their state of health, and from their professional and social activity" (*AA*, 4).

It is interesting that friendship is identified as important in lay life and in the lay apostolate (*AA*, 4). In several of the post-council lay movements, notably the Cursillo and Marriage Encounter, friendship (with Christ and with one another) has a central place. (Friendship is also the *only* relationship that Jesus holds up to the early band of followers.)

Objectives

The second chapter of the decree lists objectives of the apostolate, the overall one being the renewal of the whole temporal order. The layperson is described as "simultaneously a believer and a citizen," one for whom both church and world matter greatly. Indeed, the laity are termed "fellow workers for the truth" (*AA*, 6) and their witness of life is complementary to pastoral ministry. The decree takes the role of the laity a step further, saying that the apostolate does not consist *only* in the witness of life, but also in "preaching the Gospel" especially to non-believers (*AA*, 6).

The gospel reaches far into the various aspects of the temporal order: family, culture, economics, the arts and professions, the laws of the political community, international relations—*all* these have intrinsic value (*AA#7*).

What we see here is the affirmation by the council (again) of the inherent goodness of the world and the institutions of society, a goodness that follows from the relationship of these entities to the human person. However, both realism and historical perspective bring the council fathers, and indeed all of us, face to face with the truth that these constructs of society often have been marred by serious errors and even vices. Original sin has not disappeared from the face of the earth.

The phrase used by the council is "excessive trust" in the progress of natural sciences and technologies, a trust that perhaps unwittingly serves as a transmitter of corruption. We might term this an uncritical and even unconscious naiveté. So what can be done to restore balance and virtue? The council turns to the laity. The lay faithful, they say, can and must recognize that the renewal of the world and society is *their special obligation* (*AA*, 7). This obligation, however, is to be shared with other citizens, men and women of good will, using their skills and competencies for a renewal that respects the inherent laws of the natural world. *Apostolicam Actuositatem* is, in fact, a call to the laity to become players in Christian social action (*AA*, 7). But, like *Gaudium et Spes*, *Apostolicam Actuositatem* understands Christ's commandment of love to reach into the whole human family; it is not reserved only for Catholics nor even only for Christians (*AA*, 8).

With a kind of prescience regarding globalization, the document states that charity is global, and prosperous nations are obliged to seek out those with needs and those suffering serious distress and to console them with great solicitude (*AA*, 8).

The council eschews "grand gestures" in this matter. Rather, the laity, and indeed the whole People of God, are asked to engage in solicitude "quietly and with an unexceptional appearance," remembering that in the neighbor is the image of God. All our actions in charity are to be undertaken with the utmost respect and consideration for the other; the demands of justice are always to be kept in mind. The causes of the ills suffered by the needy are to be searched out and those causes removed, all the while maintaining a mindfulness of human dignity, which includes freedom from dependency (*AA*, 8).

Fields of Action

Where can laity exercise their responsibility for the apostolate? There are many sites and situations that can benefit from caring, dedicated action. These include not only the social milieu at national and international levels, but also youth work, the family, and church communities. The landscape imagined by the council was vast. And when the members of the council considered that, they also recognized that *women* have talents and gifts needed for this multifaceted apostolate. Was this an early call to intentionally include women in the church's mission?

In this section of the decree (the fields of action) we can again locate inspiration for lay ecclesial ministry and lay leadership, prominent signs of the times in the twenty-first century. While the decree unambiguously declares that the pastoral care of the world is a special obligation of the laity, it also maintains that the contributions of the laity *within* the church are essential. Without this *intra* commitment, the apostolate of the pastors will be significantly less effective. In rather stirring words, the decree states that laity can "refresh the spirit of their pastor and the rest of the faithful." These words seem suggestive of the type of collaborative ministry that has increasingly been recognized as critical for a vibrant evangelization and accountability in ministry (*AA*, 10).

One privileged site for the exercise of the lay apostolate is the parish, and catechetical instruction is one key ministry. The council sees this site as a doorway that enables the laity to bring their talents within the heart of the church and, in addition, to bring the problems of the larger community—the community *without*—into the heart of the church.

The vision of the council reaches beyond the parish. The diocese and the national and international expressions of the church are also in need of the experience and competencies of the laity. Thus the horizon is even larger, namely, missionary activity (*AA*, 10).

Of particular importance to laywomen and laymen is the council's focus on married persons and families—households—as actors in the apostolate. This emphasis is a faithful echo of the debate and eventual consensus that rang through the *aula* during the council deliberations. The language used regarding marriage is significant. Husband and wife are called *partners*, which, of course, implies equality, a point of view that has been central in the contemporary theology of marriage. Moreover, the household (i.e., the home) is referred to as a *domestic sanctuary*, a place of mutual affection, prayer, hospitality, and the promotion of justice and charity (*AA*, 12). The idea of the family as *the domestic church* became a centerpiece of the postconciliar theology of marriage and family.[2]

Apostolicam Actuositatem focuses on youth in terms of both concerns and expressed hopes. Youth are encouraged to be apostles and adults are encouraged to enter into meaningful conversations with youth, appealing to their ideals. While promoting inter-generational dialogue (and action), the decree also holds up the apostolate of "like to like," a method that developed in the years prior to the council (*AA*, 13).

One of the "signs of the times" is said to be the solidarity of all peoples, and a major task for the apostolate is to contribute to that solidarity.

Alone and With Others

When the various forms of the apostolate are discussed, the decree states unambiguously that the laity can engage in the apostolate as *individuals*; they need not join a group. They may, of course, but it is not necessary. What is necessary, though, is that laymen and laywomen engage in some type of apostolate. "All lay persons are called..." (*AA*, 16). As they work generously through their professions, in their families, in their cultural and social life, they are cooperating with God.

This point has special meaning when one considers the historical moment in which the council occurred. Communism was restricting individual freedom throughout large portions of the world and the laity were being urged to do whatever was possible "to take the place of priests." Specifically mentioned as roles for the laity are teaching Christian doctrine and helping people follow a sacramental way of life. Informal networks, it was noted, were one way to realize these goals.

A Croatian family I know experienced personally the value of an informal network. In the mid-1940s Melita and Mladen had been married for two years and had a year-old child when late one night a priest arrived at their home. He had come to warn Mladen that he was on Tito's death list and to tell him that he had to leave before dawn. Tito was restructuring Yugoslavia's legal system along communist lines. Mladen, a lawyer, a radio journalist, and a devout Catholic, could be seen as an obstacle.

Taking his priest-friend's advice, Mladen left his homeland, eventually making his way to America, where he learned new skills and entered a new field of work. His wife and child stayed behind. For twelve years the only communication between Melita and Mladen was written, with Mladen pretending to be a woman friend. The correspondence was in French.

Meanwhile, Melita was determined to provide her child with religious education, and to that end an informal network of committed Catholics, including priests, passed on the sacramental and doctrinal tradition. She told me that, in effect, she and her daughter "went underground" on a regular basis so that faith formation could take place.

In the late 1950s, Melita and her daughter were able to leave Yugoslavia and join Mladen in the United States. One of the life lessons she learned during those years, a lesson she has passed on by the witness of her life, is the strength of the marriage vow. She says it was a major source of inner sustenance during the difficult and dangerous years when she was alone. The other support was the community of believers, quietly keeping the faith.

Forty years have passed since the decree was approved, and communism for the most part has passed into history, but these ideas are relevant today as new forms of totalitarianism may arise.

On the other hand, while the individual apostolate was affirmed, united efforts were also endorsed by the council. Catholic Action, which in the council debates was often blended into the whole notion of the lay apostolate, is more clearly defined in *Apostolicam Actuositatem* as "collaboration of laity in the apostolate of the hierarchy" (*AA*, 20). The spirit of compromise, which can surely be interpreted as the action of the Spirit, can be seen in the "either/or" approach to Catholic Action. The lay apostolate may be participation in the hierarchy's apostolate, but the cooperation of the laity can occur "in their own way," utilizing the uniqueness of the laity's experience and with the laity assuming responsibility for their organizations (*AA*, 20). However, lest there should be a misreading of the council's intent regarding lay autonomy, it is situated in the theological construct of the church as communion. "The laity function under the direction of the hierarchy...and the latter can sanction this cooperation by an implicit mandate."[3]

It is interesting (and perhaps curious) that after de-linking, to some degree, lay organizations from Catholic Action, the document states that any organization which *in the opinion of the hierarchy* displays certain characteristics (evangelization of humankind; the sanctification of men and women; the formation of human conscience) must be considered Catholic Action, even though titles, forms, and the like may differ according to regions and peoples (*AA*, 20). This somewhat convoluted presentation reveals both the entrenchment of Catholic Action in the Latin countries, particularly Italy, and the reluctance to "canonize" that form of the apostolate on the part of other countries, particularly the English-speaking ones. Debates about Catholic Action, with its political hues, continued up to and during the synod on the laity in 1987.

Appreciation

An effort to praise the dedication of the laity is clearly found in the text, and it echoes the debate on an early draft of the document when bishops from around the world insisted, in one way or another, that the laity were generous and trustworthy and should be consulted widely. Likewise, lay associations are to be praised, states the decree, but those groups deemed most responsive "to the needs of time and place" are to receive special mention (*AA*, 21). *Aggiornamento!*

International associations receive special mention, a reflection perhaps of the international nature of the church, as do those women and men who devote themselves to such associations either permanently or temporarily. The reality of lay people laboring in the mission lands brings heartfelt appreciation. The bishops say these individuals are to be welcomed by the pastors of the church who should make sure that "the demands of justice, equity and charity... [are] satisfied to the fullest extent, particularly as regards proper support for them and their families, including necessary formal spiritual consolation" (*AA*, 22). This is an important teaching for the growing number of lay ecclesial ministers in our time.

Relationships

A general principle is laid down in the document: the spirit of unity must be promoted, and mutual esteem among *all* forms of the apostolate are to be demonstrated.

A meaningful point for the beginning years of the twenty-first century is this: many apostolic undertakings freely chosen by the laity and regulated by them are fine. This recognizes that certain needs require creative responses, possibly something quite new and different. In Part Three we will discuss a number of post-council lay movements that fit that criterion.

However, the decree is clear that no project "may claim the name 'Catholic' unless it has obtained the consent of the lawful Church authority." This is also a meaningful point for our time. Nevertheless, there is encouragement for the laity to act on their own—"they must not be deprived of the possibility" (*AA*, 24), and the procedure for granting a mandate is mentioned. The word "entrust" is used regarding laity undertaking certain pastoral duties, including that of the "care of souls." The latter technically refers to pastoral work in parishes, but one can also see in this duty the opening to spiritual direction in the life of the laity—certainly as recipients of this ancient ministry, but also as trained spiritual directors.

Called to Collaborate

All the ordained (including bishops) are reminded that the right and duty to exercise the apostolate is common to *all* the faithful, including the laity, and so the clergy are urged to work with laypersons "fraternally." How can this kind of relationship be developed? Through the devoted pastoral care of the ordained for the lay members of the church, and through continuous dialogue.

Collaboration can be made real, the council believed, through diocesan councils of various kinds, and indeed, at the level of the parish as well. There is a clear sentiment within the document for the establishment of councils to promote shared responsibility for the mission of the church (*AA*, 25).

And at the international level, there is a call for a "special secretariat" to be situated at the Holy See specifically for the promotion of the lay apostolate, and with the understanding that clergy and religious will cooperate with the laity (*AA*, 26).

Formation

The importance of the spiritual formation of the laity is a familiar refrain within the contemporary church. It was not so in 1965. Formation was believed to be for those called to religious life, or for the ordained. Therefore, the recognition that an effective apostolate is dependent on a "diversified and thorough formation of the laity" was a new insight. The document makes reference to other council documents that touch on this idea, especially *Lumen Gentium* and *Unitatis Redintegratio*, the Decree on Ecumenism (*AA*, 28). There is a clear implication that the formation should not imitate formation for religious, but should be distinctively lay. Moreover, *human* formation is given its proper place as the foundation for spiritual and theological formation, and the "art" of living cooperatively is linked with "friendly" conversations. Years later the United States bishops, in a document on the leadership of women, would endorse the notion of "dialogue that is clear, sensitive, patient and built on trust."[4] One bishop used the phrase "sacred conversations."

In an echo of the Declaration on Christian Education, the Decree on the Apostolate of the Laity looks to the family as a sort of apprenticeship for the apostolate, the place where children learn to widen their circle of concern. But educational institutions, at all levels, have a role in formation, and indeed teachers and educators, by virtue of their work, are engaged in the apostolate (*AA*, 30).

Lay groups and associations are granted the right to promote a formation suitable to the goals of the group. Small group meetings (as in the Cardign method, for example) are acknowledged as sites for doctrinal, spiritual, and practical formation. To this day, the small group or small community of faith is a prime means for the formation of the laity.

Formation is meant to lead to something—a witness of life that is non-materialistic, social concerns, works of charity and mercy—and to that end all aids should be employed. These aids include frequent meetings, spiritual exercises, study sessions, congresses, and conferences (*AA*, 31). There is no mention of laity acquiring a theological education in a seminary (as many do today), but the idea of centers or institutes for this purpose is endorsed, with the hope that the educational/formational enterprise will include anthropology, psychology,

and sociology. One is reminded of Jesuit theologian Bernard Lonergan's urging interdisciplinary centers for theological formation.[5]

Finally, the decree exhorts—*entreats*—the laity to respond to these
ideas, reminding them of Christ's invitation to come closer to Him,
"recognizing that what is His is also their own." The decree then is
basically a plea to the laity to join with Christ in His saving mission as
nothing less than His co-workers in this moment of history.

PART III

IMPLEMENTATION

The council's exhortation to the laity in *Apostolicam Actuositatem* to share responsibility for the mission of the church, including the work of education (the pursuit of knowledge) "in such a way that they not merely advance the internal renewal of the church but preserve and enhance its beneficent influence upon today's world, especially the intellectual world" (*GE*, 12) was well received in many places. The United States hierarchy, under the leadership of Archbishop John Dearden, came home from Rome committed to a serious and thorough implementation of the council's teachings—and hopes—and that included the promotion of the lay apostolate. Nor was Rome idle. The voices of bishops who emphasized that a curial presence for the laity was needed in order to ensure implementation could still be heard.

THE PONTIFICAL COUNCIL OF (AND FOR) THE LAITY

By 1967 a Council of the Laity had been established with the intent of promoting the lay apostolate as defined by the Second Vatican Council. Also of concern, however, was the need for some instrumentality to move forward the justice and peace teachings in *Gaudium et Spes*. The newly established Council of the Laity was to address both objectives, with justice and peace issues to be dealt with by a special commission associated with it. Council members were all lay: twelve men and two women. There were also consulters, both lay and clergy. Among the latter was Karol Wojtyla, who a decade later would become Pope John Paul II.

A secretariat was created with a cardinal as president, a bishop as vice-president, a priest as secretary, and two *lay* undersecretaries, one of whom was Rosemary Goldie. A woman was now in the curia! It was not exactly what the council fathers had had in mind, but it was a start, and it was considered experimental, an experiment that lasted for eight years.[1]

An example of the close alliance between Christian education and the lay apostolate could be found in a joint project of the Council of the Laity and the Congregation for Education in 1972. A group from around the world was gathered, their focus being university youth and their needs. Professors, chaplains, students, leaders of youth movements—all shared their experience, which was as rich as the global church: campus ministry in the United States; chaplaincies for foreign students in Europe; efforts to integrate the university into the Arab society in Lebanon; new political consciousness in India; the number of women students in much of the developing world; the impact of liberation theology—all these urgencies shaped the agenda of this collaborative group, which was encouraged by Pope Paul VI. And this work was taking place against the background of the student riots of the 1960s.[2]

In 1976, the Council *of* the Laity was renamed Council *for* the Laity. It did not claim to represent the whole laity of the world to the Holy See, but rather to be representative of the *diversity* of lay concerns. The members of the council were increased to twenty-five while the leadership of the secretariat remained clerical: a cardinal president, a bishop vice-president, a monsignor secretary, and lay undersecretaries along with other staff members.

The focus of the new council included youth, the vocation and mission of women, lay commitment to the world, participation of the laity in the life of ecclesial communities, and structured forms of lay participation as in councils of various kinds. The encouragement of dialogue explicitly undergirded all the programs undertaken by the Council for the Laity and the secretariat. There was also a committee on family life until 1981 when Pope John Paul II created the Pontifical Council for the Family, a year after the international synod on marriage and the family.

THE AMERICAN BISHOPS:
IMPLEMENTING THE SECOND VATICAN COUNCIL'S DECREES

John Dearden's energies initially went to a reorganization of the bishops' national headquarters. In 1966 the bishops voted to establish two entities: the National Conference of Catholic Bishops (NCCB), whose mandate was to implement Vatican II in terms of internal church life, and the United States Catholic Conference, whose focus was external relations with other institutions of society. The staff of both these "conferences" functioned under the leadership of a general secretary and eventually three associate general secretaries.[3] On the NCCB side, a number of secretariats were set up to implement different decrees of the council. Their staffs tended to be small, usually a director, occasionally an associate director, and one or two support people.

Initially, the newly organized national headquarters did not have a secretariat *of* or *for* the laity. There was, however, an ad hoc Bishops' Committee on the Laity as well as the energy to change its status to that of a standing committee (with an elected rather than an appointed chairman) that would participate in setting the national agenda along with other standing committees, such as those on Doctrine and Liturgy. And there was the desire to establish a permanent secretariat to support the committee.

The National Advisory Council

The Second Vatican Council had highlighted the value of councils at different levels of church life. These were envisioned as vehicles through which the laity could participate in decision-making according to canon law but in the true spirit of shared responsibility. One of the first initiatives, therefore, of the "Dearden administration" was to establish a national council comprised largely of laity but also with members from religious orders and the clergy, including bishops. During the first years—the late sixties into the seventies—members were appointed by the president of the conference of bishops. Many of them were stellar players on the American ecclesial stage: well-known theologians knowledgeable about the Second Vatican Council, members of learned societies, pastoral leaders, and lay leaders of national movements and organizations.

The purpose of the national council was twofold, one explicit and one implicit. The explicit purpose was to advise the Administrative Committee of bishops, which was comprised of chairmen of the standing committees and bishop delegates from the country's episcopal regions. These bishops set the agenda for the annual general meeting of the bishops, in particular regarding what actions would be taken by the whole body (e.g., statements, pastoral letters, etc.). The *implicit* purpose had to do with Cardinal Dearden's view of the first years of the National Advisory Council as a prelude to the establishment of a National Pastoral Council with elected membership, understood as a natural component of a system of councils that would include dioceses and parishes.

The Netherlands had already established a national pastoral council and its proactive positions on a number of contentious issues had brought an intervention from the Vatican: there would be no national pastoral councils anywhere. Period. And so the U.S. National Advisory Council (NAC) was confirmed as *advisory*.

After I began to work at the National Conference of Catholic Bishops (1977), I regularly attended the twice-yearly meetings of the National Advisory Council. I was impressed by the respectful exchange of different points of view about subjects of far-ranging concern: everything from liturgy, to shared responsibility for church governance, to resigned priests. Strong differences of opinion were evident but they occurred in a climate of genuine searching and common fundamental values.

During the course of one of these meetings I spoke in euphoric tones to an archbishop who had been associated with the council since its inception in 1968. The archbishop smiled and said that in the beginning, the atmosphere had been volatile with occasional shouting matches —"Those early meetings usually ended in fatigue," he added. What I was seeing, however, was that they could disagree with civility. Members were intelligent and strong willed, and while not ideological, they were convinced of the rightness of their positions. What had caused the transformation, I wanted to know. The archbishop said that change had come when the leadership of the council had rearranged the three-day meetings around prayer, socializing, and fun, in addition to the business agenda. The result was that the members got to know each other in a personal way. I'm reminded of some wisdom attributed to Bernard Lonergan, that "we meet not only to be together and to settle human affairs, but also to worship."[4] Worship has a way of leveling the field. So does fun.

CALL TO ACTION (1974–1976)

One of the more far-reaching actions taken by the National Advisory Council was the urging of a nationwide program to discern the state of the question regarding justice in the United States. This was envisioned as a contribution by the Catholic Church to the bicentennial observance of the founding of the nation. Cardinal Dearden and the conference of bishops embraced the idea, as did the NCCB's general secretary, Bishop James Rausch. As a program of the bishops of the United States, it was connected to church structures in its conception and implementation. It sought contributions from all the people of the church, laity as well as religious and clergy, and so provided a vehicle for expressing shared values and meaning. In so doing, it stirred up the desire for the experience of community within the church, a "community of faith and friendship" in the words of Cardinal John Dearden, who presided over the final event, the Detroit Conference on Justice.

For a long time the church in the United States had contended with the tensions arising from its Roman Catholic roots, deeply hierarchical, now planted and cultivated in the soil of democracy. Charges of a borderline heresy, Americanism, were still vividly present in the memory of the American bishops. European prelates remained chary of the American church's openness to the separation of church and state, and it was not until the Second Vatican Council's issuance of the Declaration on Religious Freedom—of which American Jesuit theologian John Courtney Murray, SJ, was the principal architect—that the clouds of suspicion were lifted somewhat.

Call To Action, conceived by the bishops of the United States as an all-encompassing conference on justice with the widest possible consultation with the laity about the state of the church and the state of the nation, could not have come into being without the foundational principles supplied by *Dignitatis Humanae* and *Gaudium et Spes*. The project would have remained in the realm of ideas—and hopes.

Call To Action—the name was taken from the popular title of the letter (issued May 14, 1971) of Pope Paul VI to Cardinal Roy which outlined the political and social responsibility of Catholics—was, in fact, a child of the greatest ecclesial event of the twentieth century, the Second Vatican Council. Call To Action (CTA) was a major breakthrough of historic proportions in terms of involving the People of God—the grass roots—in determining a pastoral agenda for the church in the particular culture that was America at the beginning of the last quarter of the twentieth century.

Perhaps as an acknowledgment of its indebtedness to the insights and courage of John Courtney Murray, the Call To Action sub-committee on history urged the republication of his seminal work, *We Hold These Truths*, and the Sheed & Ward publishing company followed through on the suggestion.

Awareness of the roots of American Catholicism and its courageous leaders was present throughout the preparations for CTA. Historians David O'Brien, Philip Gleason, and Robert Trisco stoked that awareness and were influential in creating a substantive context for the consultation process. Others, too, pressed the historical dimension. In 1974 Judge Genevieve Blatt, a distinguished Catholic laywoman from Pennsylvania, in a letter to Bishop James Rausch, urged the canonization of Mother Elizabeth Seton during the bicentennial celebrations. It became known as the "Mother Seton Resolution," and was intended to recognize the establishment of the Catholic school system as a part of American Church history (Elizabeth Seton was canonized in 1975).

Three Days in Detroit

The historical framework for Call To Action was also palpable as the Detroit conference began. People were aware that this was the first time in the history of the American Catholic Church that the full spectrum of membership, laity through hierarchy, would have equal voices in a plenary session. The process did not include any veto power for the bishops during the conference itself. Heightened expectations were tinged with nervousness.

Not all dioceses chose to participate in the consultation process or the Detroit conference. Chicago, with Cardinal Cody at the helm, was one. On the other hand, Peter Leo Gerety, archbishop of Newark (New Jersey) since 1974, filed into the main meeting space of Cobo Hall in Detroit as head of his diocesan delegation of nine.

The number nine had been deliberately chosen by the planners. It enabled the delegates to participate in each of the eight topic groups and allowed for an additional topic group should that be needed. The delegate formula had been well thought through. Three diocesan delegates would be from church agencies (schools, for example); three would be laypeople who had taken part in the bicentennial preparation, and three would be persons who had directly experienced injustice.

National organizations had different criteria. To participate, an organization needed to demonstrate only two things: that it was national in scope and Catholic in its identity. Furthermore, the organizations were asked to develop their own guidelines for *who* their delegates would be, and this had the potential for trouble.

Still, when Archbishop Gerety entered, he felt something powerful, something of the Holy Spirit was about to be unleashed. He had participated energetically in the preparation for this unique gathering of the church. Parishioners in the archdiocese of Newark were among the thousands of Catholic laymen and laywomen who had spoken their minds and their hearts about their own needs in these fresh postconciliar years, and about their hopes for the church they had loved long and faithfully, the church that was as close to them as their own souls. It was the people of America's parishes who had identified the concerns that were finally crafted and shaped into the major topics of the whole process (450,000 responses from across the nation had been received at the NCCB/USCC headquarters). Personhood, The Church, The Neighborhood, The Family, Ethnicity and Race, Nationhood, Humankind, and Work were the topics that emerged from one of the largest consultative processes in the history of the church.

Ursuline Sister Alice Gallin, a former professor at the College of New Rochelle (who would later become the executive director of the American Association of Catholic Colleges and Universities) was asked to coordinate this massive undertaking. With the help of college students and other volunteers, she managed to analyze the hundreds of thousands of pages of input generated by the people of the church.

Archbishop Gerety not only supported the *idea* of Call To Action, he had also been an active participant in all six of the regional hearings. Wearing an open-collared sport shirt and favorite sweater, he had listened carefully to expert witnesses, among them Alexis Herman, then an official with Catholic Charities and later a member of President Clinton's cabinet, who spoke about the situation of women in society and in the church; and Dorothy Day, who movingly witnessed to the plight of the poor. (She was also shocked to find TV cameras present.) All around the country were testimonies from union leaders, government leaders, church officials and theologians, and experts on issues concerning families and youth. These testimonies fed into Gerety's ever widening intellectual horizon and his experience as a social justice activist.

But vividly present to him too, on this opening day of the Detroit conference, were the ordinary people who testified. A disabled mill worker who described his work conditions in the Southeast; coal miners suffering from work-induced diseases; a divorced woman struggling to care for her children and to be accepted in her church community. Sometimes Gerety and others on the "listening panels" were barely able to control their tears. The divorce question, in particular, was of widespread concern. The grass-roots consultation had questioned the practice of automatic excommunication of divorced Catholics, and the regional hearings put anguished faces on the practice. Why, wondered some of the American bishops, was U.S. ecclesial law stricter than the universal law of the church? (The American bishops did, in fact, remedy the situation.)

Other issues also claimed their attention. They were touched by the plight of immigrant women living in fear of being returned to hostile environments and by the stories of family farmers on the verge of bankruptcy.

Over and over, they were struck by the havoc caused by systematic injustice. Stories of white flight in changing neighborhoods (including flight from Catholic institutions) particularly pained Gerety who had spent much of his adult life fighting racism. All his formation had included "taking a stand"; for him it was intellectual and practical, personal and spiritual.

John Cardinal Dearden, a Leader

From the moment the idea for this national celebration of justice in the world was accepted by the bishops' conference, Cardinal Dearden was committed to listening attentively to the voices of the people of God in America. "We must be true to our word," he confided to Jane Wolford Hughes, the director of Detroit's adult education program. "Without listening there can be no dialogue."

He hadn't always thought this way. As the bishop of Pittsburgh he was known as "Iron John," a nickname that described a somewhat unyielding presence. A former professor at St. Mary's Seminary in Cleveland, Father Dearden taught many future bishops. It was his custom to begin each philosophy class with a fifteen-minute presentation in Latin. Someone skilled in the ancient language would translate and pass the notes around for the next day's class. John Whelan, later archbishop of Hartford, is remembered for such generous translations. An early lesson in collaboration, perhaps?

People who knew him well say it was the Second Vatican Council that profoundly changed Dearden's way of thinking about the church and his role and responsibility within it. He was revered for bringing the teachings of the council into the organizational life of the bishops' conference. During his presidency the conference made the transition from an organization run by cardinals and archbishops to one that was more democratic and decentralized. Stories abound of Dearden's kindness to young leaders and his determination to impart to them his own enthusiasm for the Second Vatican Council.

Many applauded what might be called a conversion, but others felt differently about the change in Dearden. Jerry Filteau, long-time reporter for Catholic News Service, has never forgotten the moments just prior to the opening of the Call To Action conference. One man broke through police security in Cobo Hall and rushed at the cardinal screaming "Judas!" He was later identified as a member of an organization called Sons of Thunder, which opposed changes in the church that flowed from the council.

It is this culminating conference, charged with energy, hope, and diversity, that is generally remembered as the bishops' program, Call To Action. But the regional hearings, described earlier, were considered by the planners to be the heart and soul of the process. The hearings were suggested—and later crafted—by Francis J. Butler, who had been tapped by NCCB general secretary Bishop James Rausch to direct this ambitious consultation. Butler's Capitol Hill experience with Congressional hearings was the model for the CTA regional hearings. Butler brought more than political acumen to the project, however. He held a doctorate in theology from The Catholic University of America, and as a young husband and father of small children, he understood well the aspirations and needs of ordinary Catholics.

Pope Paul VI

As Call To Action began in Detroit, Pope Paul VI spoke to the delegates via a previously filmed presentation. "The cause of human dignity and human rights is the cause of Christ," he said. The delegates were deeply moved by the message of the seventy-nine-year-old pontiff, by his defense of life, freedom, and justice. He spoke to the bishops and to the whole people of God in language immediately identified as inclusive. "Venerable brothers and dear sons and daughters," he began, "Before the world you are humbly asserting your conviction that freedom and justice are truly essential elements of Christ's teaching, that they are primary needs of the human person, that they engender rights and duties of supreme importance." He linked the renewal of true freedom and justice in economic and social structures to "personal and interior conversion" and said that any call to action was first of all a call to prayer, that "the mark of our discipleship is concern for our brethren." This was the first time that a papal message had been relayed via modern technology, and the delegates loved it. In every way and from every quarter, from pope to parish delegate, Call To Action offered a new way of being the church in the world.[5]

The Working Groups

When the opening ceremonies and speeches were over, the really hard work of the Detroit conference began. The diocesan delegates quickly went to their "working groups." In addition to the delegates there were a thousand non-delegates, leaders and representatives from national organizations and movements, *observers*, who spoke for different segments of the church. Some were mainstream and some were considered marginal. Cardinal Dearden had argued for the presence of these various groups, saying that he had given his word that he, and Call To Action, would be in a listening stance. The Detroit organizers decided that the observers could attend the working groups: they would have voice but no vote.

Many of the observers turned up in the Personhood working group, where issues of human sexuality found a natural home. Some focused on internal church life rather than on societal ills, so questions about celibacy and a married clergy were introduced, as was women's role in the church, including ordination. *Humanae Vitae*, which had caused an uproar in 1968 with its prohibition of contraception, once again brought on heated discussion.

These were not the issues *per se* that had found their way up from the parishes into the regional hearings and onto the floor of Cobo Hall. Nor were they the issues of which Pope Paul VI had spoken so movingly in his pastoral comments to the Call To Action gathering. They were, however, the ones the media fixed on. They became the headlines, the sound bites, and the remembered story of "what happened in Detroit."

Complicating the matter was the fact that the organizers did not have a mechanism for prioritizing recommendations presented to the bishops' conference. In the end, the recommendations were disposed of as follows: (1) they were remanded to a committee of the NCCB/USCC to be addressed according to conference procedures, or (2) they were placed in a category called " for future study," or (3) they were judged to be issues for the universal church to deal with, and so outside the competence of the conference, or (4) they required action by parishes or dioceses and as such were also outside the circle of national responsibility.

The process on the floor proved to be exhilarating and exhausting. Joseph Bernardin (about to become president of the NCCB/USCC) was wary of the whole thing. Bishop Rausch, the general secretary, was ready to take the next steps. Rausch's associate general secretaries, Fathers Michael Sheehan and Thomas Kelly, OP, were not quite so sanguine. In fact, they were eager to return to Washington and to their routines.

Afterward

Like Sheehan and Kelly, the bishops, staff, and consultants—all those who had comprised the various committees that had brought Call To Action into being—had mixed and in some cases jumbled reactions to the three-day experiment in lay participation. Their ultimate goal from the beginning had been to devise a five-year pastoral plan on justice, which was to guide the work of the church in parishes, dioceses, religious communities, and church-related organizations. But, as historian David O'Brien notes, the process of open hearings, of honest and forthright discussion, of leaders *listening* "broadened the agenda considerably, as problems of pastoral care and justice within the church came to occupy an equal place with issues of justice and peace in the world."[6]

Perhaps even more important, the bicentennial committee recognized the significance of a process new to the church in the United States. The committee wrote the conference leadership, saying that it was of utmost importance that the bishops demonstrate that they had listened and cared about the sheer depth of human experience revealed through the process. Furthermore, they said, "It is important in framing a response to touch directly on the themes which lie behind and inform the specific proposals, to speak out clearly and affirmatively on the concern for shared responsibility, for renewing the life of the parish, for supporting and strengthening family life, for working to orient programs and structures to serve the real human needs which are present within and beyond the Catholic community." To that end, they recommended that the bishops issue a message to the Catholic community setting forth their response to the bicentennial consultation. They said this message "should be of a character appropriate to the extraordinary nature of the situation created by the bicentennial process. It should be marked by candor; it should be designed to continue the dialogue initiated by the program; and it should have a clearly pastoral tone, but it should not attempt to respond to the individual recommendations."[7]

The response was to be issued at the May 1977 general meeting in Chicago, and the bicentennial committee eagerly awaited it. But when Archbishop Gerety saw the document he was stunned. It had little of the flavor of a "circular model" of church, the model that had been evolving during the years of Call To Action. It had none of the tone of trusting collaboration between the ordained and the laity that had characterized these years of dialogue.

Gerety consulted with Cardinal Dearden. They agreed that a new author was needed, one who would not put his own ideological spin on the events, one whose ecclesiology was friendly to the "People of God" construct. Time was short, but within the inner workings of the bishops' conference, a hard-working theologian with a gift for prose, was willing to try. Gerety was relieved. But he still had more work to do.

In April 1977, one month before the general assembly of bishops, Cardinal Dearden suffered a serious heart attack, one that would severely limit his activity. Both he and Gerety believed that the implementation committee was composed of bishops either opposed to Call To Action or suspicious of change in any form. Behind the scenes, the archbishop of Newark quietly worked toward forming a new committee, one that was more balanced and that would include laity from the bishops' own National Advisory Council. After all, argued Gerety, it was this very council that had introduced the idea for Call To Action. He knew that without a committee of bishops and laity who understood the goals of Call to Action, this great experiment would be lost.

His plan worked. A more representative implementation committee was formed. There was still hope that the ideals and vision of this experiment in participatory church would continue on in the future.

May 1977

When the National Conference of Catholic Bishops met at the Palmer House in Chicago, a response to Call To Action was ready. Rooted in the teachings of *Lumen Gentium* and *Gaudium et Spes*, the response spoke of the value of dialogue, and of the bishops' own role as authentic teachers. While acknowledging the importance of Call To Action's consultative process, the bishops said clearly and directly that it could not be the sole factor in determining the pastoral agenda for the church. They, the bishops, would assume responsibility for the disposition of the proposals emanating from Detroit. However, they were

clearly supportive of structures for continuing dialogue and encouraged the formation of parish and diocesan pastoral councils. They
pledged to move forward on the practice of financial accountability.
They used the term "ministry" before it was part of a normative pastoral vocabulary, and before it engendered a degree of controversy in
the 1980s and 1990s.

It should be noted that the lay organization "Call to Action"
which takes its name from the bishops' original mid-seventies program, is separate in identity and goals. Some of the founders of this
organization were present at the 1976 Detroit conference and desired
to continue the "movement" toward greater lay participation. In a
short time, however, it became identified with issues like women's
ordination, and others outside the authority of the bishops' conference, and the bishops, in general, distanced themselves from it.
Another milestone happened at that May meeting. The U.S. bishops
voted to establish a Secretariat for the Laity, a step in implementing
Apostolicam Actuositatem.

A SECRETARIAT FOR THE LAITY

This new secretariat was the result of dedicated effort on the part of
Archbishop Edward McCarthy of Miami. He passionately wanted to
establish intentional and creative structures within the NCCB for liaison between the bishops and the laity of this country, both individuals
and organizations. McCarthy also wanted to find a way to encourage
meetings and dialogue among the plethora of lay groups, and he initiated a process of consultation, perhaps encouraged by Call To Action.
Committed to what he saw as a mandate from the Second Vatican
Council to enlarge and strengthen the role of the laity in the mission of
the church, he remained, even in retirement, a consistent and strong
voice for a more participatory church, and he did so with the most
unselfconscious courtesy.

When I was asked to become the first director of this new secretariat, I hesitated. It was a hesitancy born of trying to fit this "new
call" into the foundation of my life, my home and family. I constructed
lists of reasons to say Yes and reasons to say No. Then I brought my
lists and questions and doubts to a wise priest-counselor who cut

through all of them with a few words, " Trust God, and begin." The beginning was the feast of St. Francis of Assisi. I entered an empty office—no desk, no files, no paper clips—and asked the Holy Spirit to nudge me in the right direction. Memories of Call To Action lingered on at national headquarters.

Ahead lay a number of initiatives, spurred by the dynamism and hope of the bicentennial consultation: to welcome the laity into positions of responsibility for the mission of the church; to address issues of racism in the church as well as in society; to articulate the church's position on issues of war and peace (particularly concerning armaments); to develop a position regarding economic justice; to be attentive to the concerns of women in society and in the church; and to develop a theologically sound and practical plan for family ministry. All of these issues needed some kind of decisive action, all had relevance for the laity, and all reflected major themes of *Apostolicam Actuositatem*. There was enough here to keep the entire staff of the bishops' conference busily engaged for years, and so they were. But other events and issues were also stirring in 1977. Pope Paul VI was seriously ill, and there was a sense that a new papacy was about to begin.

A few months later not one, but two popes were elected—sequentially, of course. The first, John Paul I, served for only one month. His successor, John Paul II, would serve a long, long time and affect the course of twentieth-century history. A pilgrim pope, he would visit the church in the United States on a number of occasions during the final quarter of the twentieth century. During these years, laity—women as well as men—explicitly involved in various ministries would grow in numbers, and lay involvement in ministry would become a major theological conundrum and pastoral imperative. People on the margins would be seeking ways to be heard in the inner circles of pastoral care: divorced Catholics; homosexual men and women and their parents; women in violent domestic relationships; children, increasingly vulnerable and needy across the spectrum of our society. The marginalized hoped that national leaders (bishops and others) would hear their cry and respond compassionately yet realistically, setting a tone and offering practical guidance for leaders at other levels of the church, namely the diocese, the parish, schools, and social agencies.

The call from deep within the church, as well as from the margins, was for dialogue. The Second Vatican Council had given impetus to national dialogues between the Catholic Church and a number of other Christian faith communities, and these structured conversations continue to this day. Such dialogues, while quietly and carefully working toward the goal of Christian unity (the cherished hope for this third millennium), also fashioned some patterns adaptable to a number of other situations. Because so many dialogues have been under way for decades now (with Baptists, the Orthodox, Lutherans, the Reformed Churches, and the Anglican communion for example), many bishops acquired first-hand experience of how to proceed.

Furthermore, the encyclical of Pope Paul VI, *Ecclesiam Suam*, with its criteria for fruitful dialogue, deeply impressed them. The pope described dialogue as "the art of spiritual conversation" with the following characteristics:

1. *Clarity*. The dialogue supposes and demands comprehensibility.

2. *Meekness*. Dialogue is not proud, is not bitter, is not offensive, but rather is patient and generous and peaceful.

3. *Trust*, which is essential for dialogue if it is to promote confidence and friendship.

4. *Pedagogical prudence*, which strives to learn the sensitivities of the hearer and requires that we adapt ourselves and the manner of our presentation in a reasonable way.

Paul VI went on to say that the dialogue will make us wise; it will make us teachers. The "us" referred explicitly to bishops, but all church leaders, including educators, began to tap into that wisdom.

Difficult though it often is, dialogue remains an effective way to understand more deeply a number of contemporary issues. It is also a way to enter into the dynamics of conversion, particularly intellectual conversion, so necessary if there is ever to be a shift of attitude in matters of change and development. Archbishop McCarthy was in total agreement with Paul VI: dialogue, with a large measure of listening, was a path to wisdom, and a path to implementing the Decree on the Apostolate of the Laity. The question was *how* to work toward meaningful dialogue.[8]

A U.S. Council of the Laity?

In the wake of the Second Vatican Council, two national lay organizations with long and distinguished histories joined together. The National Council of Catholic Women and the National Council of Catholic Men merged into the National Council of Catholic Laity (NCCL). The model was replicated in a small number of dioceses with the hope that the trend would continue.

The NCCL maintained an office in the bishops' headquarters. For a number of reasons, however—some of them financial, some of them philosophical—that office ceased to exist. Still, volunteer leaders of the NCCL looked to McCarthy and the newly established NCCB Secretariat for the Laity to attend to some of their goals, one of which was to incorporate leadership from a variety of lay movements and organizations into levels: diocesan, deanery, and parish.

Trying to honor the aspirations of the nascent NCCL, McCarthy (and his committee of bishops and advisers) focused on convening a national conference of these different lay groups where the question of whether to continue with a National Council of Catholic Laity could be answered.

The kind of gathering envisioned by McCarthy, with national leaders from an array of lay organizations and movements covering the spectrum from left to right, was unprecedented. But, in April of 1978, four months after the new secretariat was established, representatives from more than forty groups met to try to understand one another's charisms and mission, to listen to new leaders, to express their views of the lay role in the postconciliar church. Sharing conversation and prayer, social moments and spirited discussion, were men and women from Catholics United for the Faith (CUF) and Christian Life Committees (Ignatian Spirituality); from the Judeans (a support group for divorced women who invoked St. Jude as their patron) and the newly organized North American Conference of Separated and Divorced Catholics (men and women). Organizations whose work was justice and peace mingled with those whose purpose was the promotion of quiet piety. Somehow—the grace of God—these diverse groups were able to contribute to the consultation with the Bishops' Committee on the Laity.

Toward the end of the three-day meeting, McCarthy put before the assembly two questions. First, was there a need for a National Council of Catholic Laity? The answer was a resounding No. The reasons for the negative response were not so clear. Perhaps fear of losing autonomy subsumed into an unknown "council" was one. Perhaps there was an unexpressed feeling that three days of living and working with "different others" was tolerable, but more would not be. One *expressed* reason was that the trend at the diocesan level was away from separate councils (of priests, religious laity) toward a more collaborative model: the *pastoral* council. The gathered leaders thought the new model was a way to foster understanding and collaboration for the sake of the mission. (And McCarthy was well aware that, at the national level, the National Advisory Council resembled a *pastoral* council.)

McCarthy's second question was one close to his heart. Should the Bishops' Committee on the Laity begin to develop a pastoral statement on the laity? The answer was a unanimous Yes. The archbishop had the support he felt he needed—support he wanted—to pursue the task. The only problem was that his term as chairman was drawing to a close. Still, groundwork could be laid for the next chairman.

At the final meeting of the McCarthy committee—September 1978—the bishops discussed what they believed should be the scope of the pastoral document that they intended to present as a programmatic legacy to the new chairman, whoever he might be. Key aspects included the following:

1. The pastoral statement should be short, the bishops said, an accessible document that would be read by the laity, men and women with busy, complex lives.

2. The pastoral statement should be affirming, a document that recognized the value of the laity's participation as responsible citizens of both society and church.

Short and affirming—this was the type of document the bishops wanted. The minutes show that in the deliberations they said, "We want the laity to know that we bishops stand with them, that we respect the laity, that our own ministry would be impoverished without the benefit of their experience."

There was some talk of formulating a "declaration" that would serve as a brief, powerful, affirming, truthful, readable document. And, for a while, after Bishop Albert Ottenweller's election as the new chairman, that is how the document was discussed, as a declaration on the laity. The general secretary at the time—Bishop Thomas Kelly—liked the idea.

CALLED AND GIFTED

The very first step in writing the document was for the bishops on the newly constituted laity committee to go on retreat. There they prayed and talked, mostly about how laypeople had affected their own understanding of the cost of Christian commitment, and how they wanted to acknowledge that, and to state what they believed the laity were called to, by God through the church, in the year of Our Lord, 1980—the target date for the statement.

There was a first draft followed by a consultative process. The National Advisory Council discussed it at length, and offered suggestions. The Learned Societies (e.g., the Catholic Theological Society of America, the Canon Law Society of America, the American Catholic Historical Association) looked it over. It was sent to all the lay movements and organizations.

The Laity Committee and staff sifted and sorted and wrote another draft. And that was scrutinized by a widening circle of consultants. The sending forth and reworking of the document became the rhythm of creation for the next year. It was like watching a sculptor at work, not only because a document—the one we now refer to as *Called and Gifted*—was being shaped and whittled and refined, but also because of the participation of others in the work at hand.

The bishops on the Laity Committee—Thomas Grady, Peter Rosazza, Raymond Lucker, James Hoffman, Paul Anderson, and George Evans—all had a hand in the sculpting, as did the chairman, Albert Ottenweller. They were all totally committed to the project.

In three years no one ever missed a meeting of the committee. On one occasion, one of the bishops returned from Guatemala quite sick. He alighted from the plane, jumped in a cab, and arrived at the retreat house where a two-day writing meeting was under way.

The committee was characterized by trust (they trusted God, one another, their staff, and the people they consulted); honesty (they stated their differences, and they didn't accept uncritically the suggestions that were offered); hard work; a spirit of prayer, mutual respect, and genuine affection. They came from different backgrounds; they had different work styles; their priorities were not identical, nor were their strengths and skills. One saw within the committee how different gifts and talents could be woven together to create something of meaning for others. As they sculpted, a document emerged, one whose substance was grounded in the documents of Vatican II, and it was a small piece, as originally intended. The language was non-technical, invitational, with words of belonging: bishops, laity, priests, religious—all belong to one another because all belong to Christ, and Christ belongs to God.

Called and Gifted: **What It Says**

Called and Gifted has a brief introduction and four sections identified as "calls," a term particularly close to Bishop Ottenweller who believed deeply that to be attentive to the call of God in one's life is to know joy.

The introduction establishes the foundation of the document: the role of the church as a sign of the kingdom of God. The sign is most visible, it says, when in diverse ways the church is conscious of being the People of God; and, while the document is for the whole church, the bishops highlight the laity's roles and their contributions, their gifts and how they are called to use their giftedness.

> 1. The first call is that of *adulthood*. The bishops establish this call as flowing from the Decree on the Apostolate of the Laity. "...the advance of age brings with it better self-knowledge, thus enabling each person to evaluate more accurately the talents with which God has enriched each soul and to exercise more effectively those charismatic gifts which the Holy Spirit has bestowed on all for the good of others" (*AA*, 30).

In *Called and Gifted*, adulthood is linked with interdependence. Not independence. Not dependency. Interdependence. The bishops observe in the laity many different forms of faith development, including *adult education*, through theological study and by means of theological reflection, and through experiential learning. *Called and Gifted* was implementing not only the Decree on the Apostolate of the Laity but also the Declaration on Christian Education. As people engage in the mission of the church, from evangelization to serving on committees and boards, people are formed in adult faith, the document says. It happens too in families, in the workplace, and in civic life: every struggle is formative.

2. The second call is that of *holiness*. The reference point here is the now famous article 40 of *Lumen Gentium*, which is often referred to as *"the universal call to holiness."* For the laity, says *Lumen Gentium*, the call to holiness happens in the very web of their existence (*LG*, 31). The phrase "web of existence" became the principal metaphor for describing the laity's life in *Called and Gifted*, and it perdured through every draft. The web is comprised of the events of the world, the pluralism of modern living, the complex decisions and conflicting values laity must struggle with, "the richness and fragility of sexual relationships, the delicate balance between activity and stillness, presence and privacy, love and loss."[9] We heard from people around the world who said that those lines in particular captured the heart of their human experience.

Life in the web, the bishops said, contributes to the spiritual heritage of the church. And they note how laity have sought out, for themselves, means of formation: renewal movements, guidance in prayer, spiritual direction, and what the document calls "hunger for the word of God."

3. The third call, to *ministry*, recalls the Decree on the Apostolate of the Laity on charisms and gifts being distributed in the body, with each believer having the right and the duty to use the gifts for the good of humankind and for the upbuilding of the church. Like the council's decree, *Called and Gifted* situates the laity's call to ministry in the sacraments of baptism and confirmation; the specific form of participation in ministry will vary according to the gifts of the Holy Spirit. The pivotal relationship here is clergy-laity, and solidarity between them creates an overall effective ministry and witness to the world. These comments are introductory. They are followed by several

observations about two dimensions of lay participation in ministry: ministry in the world (called Christian service), and ministry in the church, called in the document "ecclesial ministry." The world precedes the church in this arrangement to signal the importance placed on the laity's vocation in the many arenas of secular life.

There was, in 1980, considerable debate about applying the term "ministry" to civic and public activity, to the spheres of economics, business, politics, cultural development, and the like. The debate was not about whether laymen and laywomen were the church in these places; it was about language. The term "ministry of the laity" had entered church discourse largely through ecumenical discussions. It seemed to the bishops constructing *Called and Gifted* that all the churches faced a similar challenge, namely, that of connecting faith to practical issues, of being in ongoing dialogue with culture. That happens through lay presence. The Christian who goes to church, prays in private and/or in groups, ponders the scriptures, goes to work, cares for a family, and votes is one self. And that praying, spiritual self, in fact, brings the church's ministering concern to the world of microchips and the stock market and the studio and so on. Can this be called ministry? Many theologians think so.

The second aspect of the laity's ministry—service within the church —ecclesial ministry, is praised in the document. The bishops acknowledge the contributions of volunteers, of church workers (full- and part-time), including those who align themselves as a way of life with the poor. (And here they had in mind those who staff Catholic Worker houses, or those involved in similar arrangements.)

Lay participation in ecclesial ministry is not without problems. The bishops who wrote *Called and Gifted* saw that. "As lay persons increasingly engage in ecclesial ministry we recognize and accept the responsibility of working out practical difficulties such as the availability of positions, the number of qualified applicants, procedures for hiring, just wages and benefits."[10]

4. The fourth and final call is to *community*, and it is described in terms of family, the "domestic church" announced in *Lumen Gentium*. Because family is the way that people first experi-

ence community, it is decisive and pervasively influential in subsequent community enterprises. Family also influences people's expectations of the church. We read in *Called and Gifted*, "Because lay women and men do experience intimacy, support, acceptance and availability in family life, they seek the same in their Christian communities. This is leading to a review of parish size, organization, priorities, and identity."[11] The bishops go on to speak of intentional communities, forms of basic Christian communities and similar ways of revitalizing parish life as a good of the post-conciliar church.

In 1977, when I first came to the National Conference of Catholic Bishops, a synod was under way in Rome: the topic was catechetics. During my first weeks in the office, before anyone knew I was there, I had ample time to read. And I read the interventions presented at the bishops' synod that fall. Bishop Raymond Lucker spoke positively about the small community as a means of faith formation. Many Latin American bishops, too, spoke approvingly of small communities. Others, though, were not so positive. There was evident what we might call a "holy hesitancy." It is interesting, therefore, to note that the papal exhortation *Christifideles Laici*, which followed the synod on the laity in 1987, recognizes the benefits of small communities in the life of the parish.

The conclusion of *Called and Gifted* is really another call. The word is not used, but the meaning is clear: it is a call to collaboration. "The Church is to be a sign of God's Kingdom in the world. The authenticity of that sign depends on all the people: laity, religious, deacons, priests, and bishops." Then the bishops speak of listening. "We have spoken in order to listen," they say, "and we now await the next word."[12] That's the invitation to dialogue. It was an invitation eagerly accepted by lay organizations across the nation. (In the first years after approval, *Called and Gifted* was studied in many movements and organizations. And the next words were uttered indeed. Meanwhile, work began on major pastoral documents pertaining to the laity's life: on peace, on economic justice, and on women's concerns. All invited dialogue and laypeople were actively engaged in the development of these documents.)

Called and Gifted was passed on the fifteenth anniversary of the Decree on the Apostolate of the Laity: November 1980. Its passage was the result of hard work, commitment, and a great deal of prayer and patience. A miracle, some said. One bishop in particular, Bishop Albert Ottenweller, facilitated the miracle. In September 1980 Bishop Otten-weller brought the statement to the Administrative Committee of the bishops' conference with the request that it be placed on the agenda for a vote by the full body in November. As the September meeting wore on, the executives announced that the agenda was very heavy for the upcoming plenary session. Perhaps the laity statement could be post-poned, they suggested. Ottenweller countered this argument with the plea that this was an "anniversary statement": it would be fifteen years in November since the Decree on the Apostolate of the Laity had been passed. Furthermore, he said, his committee of six other bishops and four advisers had worked ceaselessly on the document. The Administra-tive Committee—about fifty bishops—listened politely, and then Otten-weller made a motion. He wanted a secret ballot to determine if the document would be placed on the November agenda. The executives were caught off balance, but before they could respond someone sec-onded his motion. The ballot motion passed and the secret vote was in favor of placing *Called and Gifted* on the November agenda.

Documents that seek approval by the entire body are open to an amendment process. In the case of *Called and Gifted*, a great number of amendments were submitted, most of them from the Committee on Doctrine and many of them expressing concern over use of the term "ministry" in relationship to the laity. The amendments sought to sub-stitute the word "service" for ministry everywhere it was used. The committee was willing to nuance one use of the term, namely, in regard to laity's role in temporal affairs—the ministry of the laity—but it was not going to change the section on church ministry. It was there that the question of women in ministry was briefly addressed. "We see the need for an increased role for women in the ministry of the Church to the extent possible. We recognize the tensions and misun-derstandings that arise on this question, but we wish to face them as part of a sincere attempt to become true communities of faith."[13] Car-dinal Krol of Philadelphia objected to that language on the grounds that it seemed judgmental of the church. His amendment failed. The bishops on the Ottenweller committee personally talked to the other bishops about their amendments, many of which were ultimately withdrawn. *Called and Gifted* passed with a comfortable margin and Bishop Ottenweller let out a cry of joy.

The tone of *Called and Gifted* was markedly different from that of other official documents. In many ways it seemed a natural heir to the debates and discussion surrounding the Decree on the Apostolate of the Laity, and indeed it was consciously rooted in the council and demonstrated a similar kind of trust. "We bishops praise the Lord for what is happening among the laity and proclaim as well as we can what we have been experiencing and learning from them."[14]

Called and Gifted was well received in diverse parts of the apostolate. As one theologian has commented, it "has been treated by all subsequent documents as a kind of blueprint for progress."[15] Indeed, in 1995 it was updated and approved once again by the general assembly of bishops, with a slightly modified title: *Called and Gifted for the Third Millennium*. This document is three times as long as the original eight-page statement. The new version retains the structure of four calls, but they are rearranged. Holiness is the first call because the writers considered it foundational for all else. Adulthood is now referred to as Christian maturity and a brief description is given of what constitutes maturity: caring for future generations, religious and theological education, respect for differences (a reflection of *Apostolicam Actuositatem*'s point that unity does not equal uniformity), participation and living with Mystery, in particular the mystery of suffering in its many forms.

The changes in the 1995 version take note of fifteen years of ongoing development and dialogue regarding the role of the laity. The 1987 Synod on the Vocation and Mission of the Laity in the Church and in the World and the subsequent papal exhortation on the Christian lay faithful, *Christifideles Laici*, as signposts of the continuing concern for lay empowerment, were understandable influences on *Called and Gifted for the Third Millennium*.

The call to ministry elaborates on church ministry and there is a pledge to support laity whose call is properly discerned in their vocation. "We [bishops] and all pastoral leaders, feel challenged to (1) develop and commit resources necessary to help laity, both paid staff and volunteers, prepare for church ministry" and "to practice justice in the workplace and to provide a living wage."[16] These and other similar pledges were made by the bishops before the monetary situation of many dioceses had been compromised by sex abuse scandals and ensuing lawsuits.

As in the earlier version, the importance of the daily life of Christian women and men not directly engaged in ecclesial ministry is recognized. "Through the sacraments of baptism, confirmation and eucharist every Christian is called to participate actively and co-responsibly in the Church's mission of salvation."[17] And, as in the case of the original statement, *Called and Gifted for the Third Millennium* invites all members of the church—laymen and laywomen in secular or consecrated life and the ordained—to continue the dialogue with one another and with the bishops.

THE 1987 SYNOD ON THE LAITY

In between these two pastoral statements on the laity there was a con-sequential Roman synod in 1987 on the Vocation and Mission of the Laity in the Church and in the World. The American delegates, elected by the bishops' conference, were Archbishop John May, Cardi-nal Joseph Bernardin, Archbishop Rembert Weakland, and Bishop Stanley Ott, who was chairman of the Laity Committee at the time. They decided to undertake a many faceted national consultation to help them focus on the questions, issues, and needs of the laity in the United States as perceived by the laity themselves. It was an ambitious plan and one that kept the secretariat fully engaged for more than a year.

Consulting the Laity

A questionnaire was designed for parishes and sent to diocesan con-tacts for distribution. Basically the questionnaire sought information about what was helping people in their efforts to be active members of the apostolate, what they needed from the church to more faithfully live out their vocation, how they experienced the workings of the Spirit in their personal and corporate lives, and what their hopes for the synod were. Some parishes held town-hall type meetings, some utilized their parish councils to probe these questions, some simply left the questionnaires in the pews with mailing labels directed to the secretariat. This grass-roots consultation gave us the initial content for further consultation.

The elected delegates met with representatives from dioceses in four regional meetings, the purpose of which was twofold: to prioritize the concerns raised in the parishes, and to enable the delegates to benefit from face-to-face conversations with laywomen and laymen. So successful were the diocesan gatherings that one for lay movements and organizations was also held.

In addition, I sought input from the readers of diocesan newspapers through two columns of inquiry. The first asked for people to write to me about how they experienced God in everyday life. These letters, which numbered in the hundreds, many of which were long and thoughtful accounts of spiritual journeys, echoed much of what we had learned from the parish and diocesan consultations. People wrote of the family as the primary place where they experienced God and this was true no matter what the configuration of the family: one parent, two parents, stressful situations. There were stories of love and loss, to use the language of *Called and Gifted*. The parish was frequently mentioned as a place where one could find meaning, and many spoke positively of the preaching (which had so often been criticized). Nature, one's work, and direct compassionate care of others, including social action, also rose to the top.

The second column put a spotlight on the workplace. Inspired by *Apostolicam Actuositatem* perhaps, we wanted to know if engaging in different kinds of work offered a way to encounter Christ. Again we were surprised at the number of respondents and the quality of their reflections. These writers ranged from those in the medical professions to supermarket workers, artists, judges, teachers, furnace cleaners. One letter has long lingered in my memory. A house painter and his wife discussed the article and she wrote a response for her husband. He told her that when he made a room beautiful with fresh paint he felt like he was cooperating with God. And when his boss told him to "cut corners" by doing one coat when the customer had paid for two, and he applied the second coat anyway, he felt that he was abiding by ethical principles. Again, his inner pull was to cooperate with God, what theologians call "actual grace." We estimated that the entire consultation involved a quarter of a million lay faithful who took the time to note the signs of the times and signs of God among us.

The bishop delegates paid attention. They chose their topics to present at the synod from the experience and insights of the laity. When the pope appointed two additional delegates, Archbishop Roger Mahony of Los Angeles and Bishop Anthony Bevilacqua of Pittsburgh, they too chose topics from the list of priorities, namely family life (Bevilacqua) and lay ministry (Mahony).

The Synod in Rome

The two topics that drew the most attention at the Synod on the Vocation and Mission of the Laity in the Church and in the World were "Women" and "Lay Ministry," topics that had stirred anxiety during the debate on the first *Called and Gifted* in 1980. The Americans had been pressing strongly for a number of years for permission to have girl altar servers; and for a number of years, opponents had been exerting a different kind of pressure. This issue was evident all around the edges of the synod, as was concern over the usage of "ministry" in relation to the laity. In fact the issues were joined. There was anxiety about the role of women in the burgeoning lay ministries around the world.

The elected delegates from the United States had published an article in *America*, under all their names, identifying the topics they would present in their eight-minute interventions at the synod. This was unprecedented. Synods, like so many other ecclesial events, preferred a totally confidential atmosphere *before*, *during*, and to some extent *after* the synods. But the delegates in 1987 wanted to honor the national consultation. The article was a way of reporting to the laity who had generously shared their thoughts, desires, and experiences of church life. The topics "Parish Life," "Political Participation," "Spirituality," and "Women in the Church" were among the issues that were uppermost in the minds and hearts of the people. So too was "Ministry," but Archbishop Weakland, who chose "Women" for his intervention, wove the ministry question into his speech. And, as indicated above, Archbishop Mahony chose to speak about ministry using the curious title "Lay Ministry: An Oxymoron." The nub of his argument was that ministry is an inappropriate term for laity. Interestingly, in the years since the synod, Mahony has issued several pastoral letters to the archdiocese of Los Angeles that reflect an expansion of his earlier thinking regarding lay ecclesial ministry.[18]

The place of lay movements was a central debate of this synod. Some wanted the movements (and they were thinking of the newer ones like Communion and Liberation) to have a certain autonomy in dioceses. On the other hand, a number of bishops wanted to be sure that these movements were operating in concert with the local church. An early proposition was worded in this manner: the lay movement is to receive permission from the Holy See or the diocesan bishop. The small word, *or*, was immediately perceived by Cardinal Bernardin as problematic. He submitted a modification, substituting *and* for *or*. The modification was accepted, much to the relief of a number of bishops. What the change assured was the preservation of local authority over the movements.

Present at the synod were lay auditors, most of whom were associated with movements, although not all; and there were also theologians, some of whom were women. As noted earlier, one auditor, Patricia Jones, a pastoral worker from Liverpool, England, was selected to address the synod. She spoke about the spiritual formation of the laity and the importance of small faith communities in that formation. So moved were the synod fathers by her presentation that their subsequent interventions frequently quoted her. One thinks of how the laywoman and economist Barbara Ward had not been permitted to address the Second Vatican Council about the world's poverty—"the time is not right yet for a woman"—and how less than a quarter of a century later "the time was right." Progress is measured perhaps in inches and hours, but it is progress nonetheless.[19]

Other auditors included some founders of new movements, notable among them Jean Vanier, whose L'Arche Movement has created communities for those with mental and physical disabilities, and Chiara Lubich, founder of the Focolare and winner of a Templeton Award for fostering ecumenical and interreligious cooperation.

After the Synod

Pope John Paul II issued two documents that engaged the topics of the synod. One was the official response, the exhortation *Christifideles Laici*, which translates into a much longer English title: The Vocation and the Mission of the Lay Faithful in the Church and in the World. The Latin title is preferable and it is more frequently used.

The exhortation gathers together many of the topics touched on in the synod, and in that way is faithful to the synod discussions. (There is always a great deal of justifiable criticism about how controlled synod proceedings are.)

In the section on the parish, one can see the heart of Archbishop John May's intervention, which, drawing on what he had learned from the national consultation, endorsed the formation of small faith communities in the parish as a means of spiritual growth and also as a means of evangelization and mission. Local ecclesial authorities are urged to foster "small, basic, or so called living communities where the faithful can communicate the Word of God and express it in word and love to one another" (*CL*, 26).

Christifideles Laici also promotes a positive definition of the term "laity" (an echo of the council), the establishment of diocesan and parish councils as instrumentalities of lay participation. It touches on family life, youth, and life in the world.

Laity are encouraged to participate in politics and government, and *Christifideles Laici* applauds those who use their gifts in service of the common good. It cites article 75 of *Gaudium et Spes* in praising the men and women who undertake the burdens of public office.

Themes from *Gravissimum Educationis* appear. We are reminded that while parents are the primary educators of their children, "a task for which they are given the grace by the Sacrament of Matrimony" (*CL*, 34), all the baptized have the right to systematic catechesis.

Regarding lay people in ministries, *Christifideles Laici* reiterates the theological teachings of the council, namely that laity participate in the priestly, prophetic, and royal office of Christ. Three sacraments are named as foundational for lay participation in various ministries: baptism and confirmation—these were underscored in the council debates and in *Apostolicam Actuositatem*, no surprise there—and in addition, ("for a good many ministries"), matrimony. The exhortation makes clear, however, that these sacraments do not make pastors of the laity; that role is reserved for the ordained.

It should be no surprise that *Christifideles Laici* seeks to comment on the role of women in society and in the church since it was such a flashpoint during the synod discussions. Furthermore, it was generally known that the U.S. bishops' conference had been working on a major pastoral letter on the concerns of women, and there was some curial anxiety about what direction it might take. This anxiety emanated both from the Pontifical Council on the Laity, where issues concerning women were, for the most part, located, and more discretely from the Congregation for the Doctrine of the Faith, where responsibility for questions regarding ordination was lodged. The exhortation is unequivocal in affirming the equality of women and men. The personal dignity of women is underscored and women are urged to reject discrimination. Regarding participation in the church's mission, *Apostolicam Actuositatem* is recalled: "...it is important that they participate more widely in various fields of the apostolate" (*AA*, 9). Interestingly, it references Pope John Paul II's apostolic letter *Mulieris Dignitatem*, which the pope termed a meditation on the dignity of woman, and which was published before the apostolic exhortation that was the fruit of the synod on the laity. Indeed, *Mulieris Dignitatem* reads like a meditation on recurring papal themes: personhood, the gift of self, equality, and diversity. There is a great deal of the spousal imagery that was a favorite of John Paul II, and in the document he expresses gratitude for "the feminine genius," a phrase that would recur seven years later during a series of papal statements directed toward the UN's celebration of the Year of the Woman. Why was there Vatican concern about the American pastoral letter on women? From the beginning it was recognized as different from other statements produced by the United States bishops.

THE PASTORAL LETTER ON WOMEN:
ITS HISTORY AND BEYOND

The little known story of how the women's question has moved forward in the church can be summarized in a few words: a number of bishops devoted their energies to change. One of them was Michael McAuliffe.

Michael McAuliffe, bishop of Jefferson City, found himself appointed chairman of the U.S. bishops' ad hoc Committee on Women in Society and in the Church in 1975 because of a mistake. His own interest lay in priestly vocations, and he had let the conference leaders know he would be willing to chair that committee. He also let his friends know.

But when McAuliffe arrived in Washington, DC, for the November 1975 general assembly of bishops, he learned that he was not a candidate for the vocations post. The conference leadership, however (Joseph Bernardin was president), did not forget about him. The relatively new Committee on Women was without a chairman (Bishop Leo Byrne, the first chairman, having suddenly died), so Bernardin approached McAuliffe, who had after all "volunteered," albeit for a different committee. McAuliffe was shocked. Like Plato's wise man, (i.e., Socrates) McAuliffe knew what he didn't know. Having grown up in a family of six boys and having wanted to be a priest from the first grade, McAuliffe knew he didn't know much about women.

Bernardin opined that McAuliffe's doctorate in the theology of marriage surely counted for something. Didn't he have a pastoral interest in family life? Well, said Bernardin, that's a fine portfolio for the women's post! McAuliffe's innate sense of loyalty, combined with his respect for justice and fairness, made accepting Bernardin's invitation that much easier.

The McAuliffe committee quickly formed (Bishops Frank Murphy and Thomas Grady among them) and decided that its first agenda item was to study the merits of the Equal Rights Amendment (ERA), bubbling up once again in the aftermath of the Vietnam War. For the next two years the committee studied all aspects of the amendment and decided unanimously to recommend public support of the initiative. Members argued (only five years after the *Roe v. Wade* decision) that abortion and the ERA were two separate issues, hence, attempts to join them were baseless. In the meantime, however, the conference leaders had consulted John Noonan, a lawyer known for his scholarly writings on the intersection of church and state in areas like divorce, contraception, and abortion. Noonan believed that abortion rights advocates would be strengthened by passage of the ERA.

Before McAuliffe began his presentation to the Administrative Committee in Chicago in May of 1978, Bernardin approached him with compliments about the fine job he was doing on behalf of the bishops, but confided that he could not support him on this matter. McAuliffe looked around the room, eager for some sign of moral support. One of his best friends, the late Bishop John Sullivan of Kansas City-St. Joseph, appeared to be earnestly studying his papers. No eye contact there. McAuliffe was on his own.

The result? The Administrative Committee unanimously voted against the recommendation of the Committee on Women, but the president and vice-president of the conference (John Quinn and John Roach) released to the press *both* reports (by the Women's Committee and the Administrative Committee). The result was this: the world beyond the meeting room in Chicago knew about the internal debate, which had probably encouraged some bishops to individually support the ERA, but to no avail. General support for the ERA around the country had faded away by that time.

Women's Ordination Conference: A Dialogue

The ERA was no sooner put to rest than Archbishop Quinn asked the McAuliffe committee to set up some form of dialogue with a new entity, the Women's Ordination Conference (WOC). "We have to listen," Quinn said. "Let us know what's being said, and what the issues are, and report to the bishops."

The bishops' committee and the WOC set up three structured dialogues with the agreed-upon goal being "to discover, understand, and promote the full potential of women as persons in the life of the Church." The conclusions reached through these intense and serious meetings fell into four categories: (1) conclusions mutually acknowledged, (2) conclusions mutually agreed upon, (3) areas of disagreement, and (4) areas for further development, with the implication of future dialogue. After each dialogue-meeting, Bishop McAuliffe dutifully reported to the Administrative Committee, which consistently expressed appreciation of his committee's work.

The final report came in the early eighties and concluded with words from Pope John Paul II in his 1979 homily at Grant Park: "Love is the power that gives rise to dialogue, in which we listen to each other and learn from each other. Love gives rise, above all, to the dialogue of prayer in which we listen to God's word, which is alive in the Holy Bible and alive in the life of the Church. Let Love then build the bridges across our differences and at times contrasting positions...." The WOC dialogues concluded on a note of hope.

For a second time, however, the Administrative Committee did not support the request of the Committee on Women. Permission to publish the substance of the dialogues was denied and no future dialogues were planned. There was, however, discussion on alternative approaches: a workshop for bishops and perhaps even a pastoral letter.

Women and the Diaconate

Meanwhile, the McAuliffe committee, indefatigable, worked on. The bishops on it had faithfully approached each task and managed to deal with their disappointments. But what now? They tried to stir up interest in a study of whether women could be ordained deacons. This idea had the support of the Committee on the Diaconate (or at least the chairman at the time, John J. Snyder) and the National Council of Catholic Women, but not many others. On visits to Rome, McAuliffe would raise the question, Why couldn't girls be altar servers? (as did many, if not most, other American bishops), still conscious of obligations of leadership. But he sensed he was getting tired.

He had a talk with himself about the need for new ideas and a fresh approach. Then he went on retreat with his friend Bishop Sullivan, and just as he had talked to himself, he talked to his friend. He was looking for discernment. Sullivan got right to the point, "It's time to resign," he said. McAuliffe concurred.

In retrospect, Michael McAuliffe is glad things turned out the way they did, that his friends forgot to nominate him for the Vocations Committee. "By doing, you learn to trust," he says. "I learned to trust." Until his death McAuliffe continued to care deeply about vocations, believing that priests have to give themselves with their whole mind, whole heart, whole self to God's people. That, in fact, is what he did when he was handed the leadership of the Committee on Women in Society and in the Church.

Bishop Joseph Imesch: Shepherd of the Pastoral

When he was asked to succeed Michael McAuliffe as chairman of the Committee on Women, Joseph Imesch, like his predecessor, protested that his knowledge of women was nil. He too, was persuaded to serve for three years. Looking back he says, "I didn't have the sense to see the pastoral letter was right around the corner." When the administrative process moved the pastoral forward, John Roach, who was now president of the bishops' conference, asked Imesch also to chair the committee tasked with writing the pastoral. Of Swiss background, Imesch has always been attracted to mountains, so the proposed pastoral, with its high ascents and steep declines, was an attractive challenge. But he never imagined it would take nine years. When the project was over, another bishop on the writing committee commented that in the history of the world, nine years was not a lot of time. "That may be so," replied Imesch, "but in the history of my life, it's a huge portion."

The project was also an enormous agent of change. Those nine years of listening to women's stories, learning about their hopes and sorrows, identifying their needs, brought Imesch to a point from which there was no turning back. The experience made him a different person, a committed advocate for women. "When I listened to their stories, I saw things differently," he says simply.

For several years he bore the dual responsibility for the ordinary work of the Committee on Women, which had become a standing committee, and the specific task of the writing committee. That would not have been possible without the skill and pastoral acumen of Sister Mariella Frye, chief staff person for both committees. A Mission Helper of the Sacred Heart and a nationally known catechist (she had attended the 1977 synod on catechetics as a *perita* to the American delegation, shattering one of the church's glass ceilings), Frye was perfect for the task. She had staffed the WOC dialogues, which had brought her into contact with the developing feminist theology. Furthermore, she was blessed with a large supply of common sense, patience, humor, and an extraordinary capacity for organization.

Early on, Imesch knew he needed a writer with knowledge of the church, one whose style would be more inviting than that of "classic magisterial," someone with a deep and abiding spirituality to sustain her through the highs and lows of the pastoral letter (and he knew it had to be a "her"). He contacted Susan Muto, a lay theologian who for many years had collaborated with Father Adrian Van Kamm at Duquesne University in Pittsburgh. She was famous for bringing literature into dialogue with spiritual theology, and much of her scholarly work had centered on Teresa of Avila, mystic and common-sense doctor of the church. A graced triad was complete.

When the first draft—"Partners in the Mystery of the Redemption"—appeared, it didn't look like other pastorals. It started with the voices of women, followed by church teaching, and then the bishops' response to the interaction between experience and tradition. Sister Joan Chittister, OSB, commented, "With 'Partners,' something different is going on." Indeed it was.

That "something different" did not last. There were rumblings about the name, the process, and the format. Opponents claimed that a new sin had been introduced, the sin of sexism. Bishop Imesch was called to Rome for a consultation with other bishops. He was joined by Bishop Matthew Clark, a member of the writing committee, and Susan Muto and Sister Mariella. Three more drafts incorporated changes (changes that alarmed the progressive bishops). By the time the final draft was presented to the bishops' meeting in November 1992, it was clear that while a majority would vote for the pastoral, this would still fall short of the two-thirds vote necessary for passage.

When Imesch stood before the assembly, the strain of "mountain climbing" was evident. He had already suffered one heart attack, but he summoned his energy and his irrepressible humor for the final presentation. "We know this fourth draft has shortcomings," he said. "It has been called overdone, underdone, or fatally flawed. On the bright side, we have helped to make *anthropology* a household word among the bishops." Then he spoke from his heart. "How history will judge our efforts during these past nine years may be disputed. What cannot be disputed is the fact that women have very deeply felt and legitimate concerns—concerns that range from abuse at home, less than equal standing in society, and in many ways, less than equal standing in the Church. Women need to know that we will not dismiss their concerns just because we cannot agree upon the appropriate response . . . women also need to hear our words translated into action." Those final words were the legacy he left to the chairmen who would succeed him after the defeat of the pastoral, the only pastoral to suffer that fate in the history of the conference of bishops.[20]

Bishops Matthew Clark, John Snyder, and John Dunne: Moving Forward

Bishop Matthew Clark, a member of the pastoral writing committee, followed Imesch as chairman of the standing Committee on Women. His first project was a national symposium for women from all the dioceses. Addressing the gathering, which was held in 1990, he shared his own experiences of *conversion*, beginning in Rome, where he had earlier served as spiritual director for the North American College, and continuing with his appointment as bishop of Rochester. It was a deeply personal and moving story of coming to consciousness. Months later, the symposium proceedings were published and *America* magazine likened the publication to the correspondence between St. Ignatius and various women of his time: daughters of Charles V, parents of Jesuits, nuns, spiritual friends. Women across the country were given hope that their ecclesial leaders and they could live in a community of faith, hope, love, and shared mission.

While the bishops were turning down the pastoral, they enthusiastically embraced a project of the Clark committee, crafted in collaboration with the Marriage and Family Life Committee: a short statement announcing the church's stand against domestic abuse. That statement has become a model for churches around the world of how to pastorally engage this particular and pervasive form of violence. It was revised in 1992.

In 1994, Clark was succeeded by Bishop John Snyder of St. Augustine. Snyder and his committee developed a response to *Ordinatio Sacerdotalis*, a difficult task, but one to which the Brooklyn native was deeply committed. *Ordinatio* had reaffirmed the prohibition against the ordination of women. The response, a relatively brief pastoral statement, *Strengthening the Bonds of Peace*, was approved by the entire body of bishops in November 1994. It called for identifying *all* the leadership roles open to women that do not require ordination. And it broke some new ground. Feminism is not demonized and sexism is named, once and for all, as sinful. Furthermore, it contains a call to study the relationship of holy orders to the power of jurisdiction.

St. Joan's Alliance, an advocacy organization begun in England early in the twentieth century to focus on promoting the role of women in the church (including ordination), used to give out buttons bearing this message: No More Studies. They had even brought the buttons to Rome during the council. When Bishop John Dunne succeeded to the chairmanship of the Committee on Women in 1996, those buttons were no longer being passed out, but something of the message lingered. Dunne probably never saw the buttons, but he had heard Imesch years before urging that words be turned into action and he may have had them in mind as he pressed for some kind of concrete action to implement *Strengthening the Bonds of Peace*.

At first the Dunne committee was interested in a pastoral plan of action, but it quickly became clear that the bishops were weary of plans as well as of pastoral letters. Instead they wrote a follow-up statement to *Strengthening the Bonds of Peace*. The new statement, *From Words to Deeds*, was issued in 1999 and it emphasizes the need for and the benefits realized from women in church leadership. Furthermore, it was and is a poignant reminder of Imesch's parting words seven years earlier that "women need to hear our [bishops'] words translated into action." These various chairmen of the Committee on Women were committed to a continuing agenda.

Feminism: Its Meaning and Its Influence

Underlying these different efforts was the question and challenge of feminism. Certain groups in the church felt the term was so tainted (because of association with abortion in the secular realm) that it could not be used with integrity in church documents. On the other hand, some of the most creative theology in the late twentieth century was feminist, coming from theologians trained in fields of scripture, systematic theology, church history, and canon law. They introduced a feminist method of inquiry into the study of theology.

Feminist theologian Sandra Schneiders, IHM, speaks of three forms of feminism. The first is *liberal feminism*, which she says is the most common. It is concerned with obtaining and assuring full equality of women in all systems in which they participate: family, the workplace, civil society, and in the church, there claiming baptism as the source and rationale. For liberal feminists, she states, this includes equal access to all seven sacraments and to positions of leadership, including those traditionally tied to ordination. Note: liberal feminists do not seek to change systems so much as to have access.

The second form is that of *cultural* or *romantic feminism*. Here, according to Schneiders, the key term is *complementary*, meaning that men and women each have an irreplaceable contribution to make to the human enterprise arising from their diverse natures. Furthermore, they must not enter each other's spheres or attempt to exercise each other's roles.

A number of feminist theologians associate John Paul II with this definition of feminist, and indeed, the late Holy Father did refer to himself from time to time as a feminist. It should be noted that the American bishops in various statements do not separate roles severely as this definition does. For example, in *Follow the Way of Love*, a pastoral statement on marriage, the bishops use the term "mutuality" and say it is about sharing power. While they recognize and appreciate diversity, they do not assign certain qualities to women and others to men, but rather acknowledge role flexibility.

The third form described by Schneiders is *radical* or *transformative feminism*. It is this form which Schneiders believes holds the most promise for reform in the church. By "radical" she does not mean fanatical, extremist, sectarian, or aggressively militant. Rather, she goes to the etymology of the term, which means root. And the root of the problem, she holds, is patriarchy, a structural problem, not a personal one, although aspects of the problem do get expressed personally. The radical feminist is not concerned so much with sexist language or the exclusion of women from full sacramental life. She is concerned with the ideology and social system that give rise to these particular evils. This comprehensive ideology is located in women's appropriated experience of sexual oppression. Schneiders contends that people *become* feminist as they move out of the patriarchal ideology in which all of us, women and men, have been socialized and into a feminist ideology by a process known as consciousness raising. This process is not so much a matter of political commitment as of conversion, a change of consciousness, something quite familiar to those exposed to Ignatian spirituality. The intellectual conversion implied here proposes a critique not of the Catholic faith but of patriarchal ideology.

Because of these feminists' adherence to the Catholic tradition, Schneiders suggests the term "feminist Catholics," with feminist being the adjective. This seems appropriate when considering the large numbers of women in critical leadership positions in the church.[21]

These women exercise leadership in a variety of settings. The late Catherine Mowry LaCugna pointed out that there is now a critical mass of Catholic women with doctorates in theology, canon law, scripture, pastoral theology, ethics, and liturgy. These theologians teach in seminaries, colleges and universities, and pastoral institutes, where they are educating future ministerial leaders: bishops, priests, and lay ecclesial ministers. Feminist Catholics are also in diocesan positions, some as chancellors with canonical authority, some as finance directors, some in charge of entire school systems or various diocesan agencies. They have introduced the feminist method of inquiry into the circles of Catholic leadership.

LaCugna (herself a theologian) pointed out that while Protestant churches routinely ordain women, fewer Protestant women pursue advanced degrees in theology. The irony that follows is that because the Catholic Church does *not* ordain women, women move beyond the final degree required for ordination, namely the Master of Divinity, to the doctoral level. Therefore, most feminist theologians are Roman Catholic and, according to LaCugna, the politics of the Catholic Church have done more than anything else to advance theological feminism as an intellectual movement and cultural force, with a huge, sophisticated and growing body of literature.[22]

In recent years, the American bishops have encouraged dialogue among women church executives. They conducted a survey of the period 1995 through 1998 about women's leadership in dioceses. Half of the dioceses in the country participated and the results showed that women hold approximately one-quarter of top diocesan positions and 40 to 50 percent of middle management positions. The Bishops' Committee on Women made the results available, and then in March 2001 they invited these church executives, exercising a variety of roles, to a meeting in Chicago to discuss the data. The women who came did so with the backing of their bishops and they spoke with the authority that comes from competence, experience, and wisdom. I attended this meeting and the voices I heard there were those of hopeful realism.[23]

Building on this work, the committee has lately explored the shape and depth of spirituality experienced by women in the workplace, not only in "church places" but secular ones as well.

LAY ECCLESIAL MINISTRY: A NEW REALITY

As indicated in Part Two, neither *Apostolicam Actuositatem* nor *Gravissimum Educationis* dealt directly with laywomen and laymen giving themselves full time to ministry within the church. More precisely, the terminology is not that of ministry. There is affirmation, however, of laity engaged in various missions: *Gravissimum Educationis*, for example, declares that teaching, in both Catholic and public schools, should be considered a true vocation. In fact, it offers a direction and encouragement for the development of a theology of work. In *Apostolicam Actuositatem* we see the clear articulation of the theological foundation for the contemporary phenomenon of lay ecclesial ministry, namely, that laity share in the priestly, prophetic, and royal office of Christ. While the Decree on the Apostolate of the Laity did not provide a blueprint for the shape and trajectory that lay ministry would follow in the post-conciliar years, it did, however, lay a strong foundation upon which the Holy Spirit could create structures appropriate to the needs of the world and the mission of the church.

Now, forty years later, the United States bishops have officially recognized that the church can benefit from guidelines for formation of these new ministers and approved a set of recommendations.[24] That moment was the result of careful work over a number of years by a sub-committee of the Bishops' Committee on the Laity, the sub-committee on Lay Ecclesial Ministry. This sub-committee sponsored hard research on lay ministry in parishes and learned that as recently as 2004 there were thirty thousand laywomen and laymen serving as paid parish ministers. In addition, the sub-committee organized theological colloquia on developments in ministry, and they published the results of their research and study. At every stage, bishops have been invited—urged even—to bring to the conversation their pastoral concerns and experience, making the work of the sub-committee truly a service to the entire church.

These conversations stressed the importance of collaboration among all those in ministry—ordained, vowed religions, and lay. As one cardinal archbishop wrote: "As laypersons assume positions of parish leadership, perhaps nothing is more important than cultivating, nurturing and sustaining collaboration between and among priests, deacons, vowed religious, and lay leaders. Such collaboration is more readily assured as each one has a clear sense of the distinctiveness and particularity of his or her vocation, recognizing the importance of bringing different gifts to bear in the common mission of the church."[25] This emphasis finds its origin in both *Apostolicam Actuositatem* and *Gravissimum Educationis*.

These doctrinal and pastoral developments in lay ecclesial ministry are likely to be studied and evaluated next to the exhortations that emerged from the 2005 synod on the Eucharist, and by implication, the eucharistic community.

Lay Movements and Organizations

As we have seen, lay movements have been a powerful force in moving laity to the center of the church's self-understanding. Much of the ferment prior to the council originated in lay movements of different kinds. The Second Vatican Council not only affirmed the known movements and organizations, it gave birth to a number of new ones. Interestingly, several of those originated in Spain.

The Cursillo Movement has had and continues to have a huge impact in the United States. The same can be said for Marriage Encounter which followed Cursillo in the post-council period. Both of these movements have sparked variations, like Teens Encounter Christ and Engaged Encounter.

In the years immediately following the close of the council, Opus Dei was usually categorized as a lay movement, and as such was invited to consultations and conferences with the Bishops' Committee on the Laity. Since becoming a prelature of the church, its status with regard to the Committee on the Laity and the secretariat has been somewhat changed. As a prelature, Opus Dei resembles a trans-geographic diocese more than a lay movement.

Perhaps the most creative movements are those that have drawn on "theology from below," to paraphrase the liberations theologians. These movements have been largely founded by laity (in contrast, say, to the Spanish movements mentioned above) and are grounded in corporate prayer, either the liturgy of the hours or the Eucharist. In addition, care for the poor in some sustained and intentional way is central to these movements. The concept of "community" best describes them. One of these "new communities" is San Egidio.

The San Egidio community started in 1968 in Rome, when a young man sat in the then run-down church of San Egidio and asked the Holy Spirit to guide him in his life. Some other young people joined him in prayer, and together they waited for God. A direction became apparent to them; they felt drawn to evangelize and to work with the poor. They began to reach out to children in need, visiting abandoned children living in institutions in Rome and teaching Gypsy children living in camps outside the city. The community found a creative solution to the problem of teaching Gypsy children. Instead of trying to make the children come to conventional classrooms (an approach that had had little success), they went to the Gypsy camps and taught them in abandoned buses there.

The community of San Egidio has grown over the years. It now has about fifteen thousand members, located in Rome and in other cities in Europe, North and South America, and Africa. Members do not formally join; they commit themselves to live the San Egidio vocation: faithful listening to the gospel in prayer, both personal and liturgical; prompt service to the poor; and support and care for one another.

These people have also committed themselves to peace-making. They helped organize the Prayer for Peace Day in 1986, an inter-religious prayer event, and have been involved in peace negotiations in many warring countries. The community has been nominated several times for the Nobel Peace Prize.[26]

Other organizations were formed in response to pressing pastoral needs which became evident in the years following the council. The North American Conference of Separated and Divorced Catholics, begun in 1975, creates networks of support for families experiencing separation and divorce; Rainbows was founded to provide emotional support for children and adolescents grieving because of death or divorce;

Retrouvaille exists to heal troubled marriages. These are examples of organizations designed to minister to contemporary families.

In the 1970s and 1980s the Bishops' Committee on the Laity regularly consulted and dialogued with a wide range of lay movements and organizations. The USCCB Secretariat for Family, Laity, Women and Youth keeps in touch with these groups and publishes, on a regular basis, a directory of more than one hundred recognized national lay movements and organizations. The directory is organized into three broad categories: (1) Lay Movements, defined as groups established by the laity with a specific charism or area of focus; (2) Professional Associations whose members come from specific professions such as youth ministry or education; (3) Organizations, which are typically Catholic non-profit organizations that do not easily fit into the other two categories. Other groups of laity—secular institutes, third orders, and pious associations—are not included in the directory, although it provides information on how to learn more about them. Part Four of this volume, "The State of the Questions," will touch on some of the most recent lay initiatives and their potential influence in light of our present historical moment.

Laity in Ecumenical Dialogue

When the council closed, doors opened to ecumenical dialogue, many of them being "dialogues of life," or informal interactions grounded in daily living. Christians from different churches joined together in common cause: fair and open housing, peace with justice, care for the earth. Catholics were among them. Some crossed the thresholds of one another's homes for structured conversations about their belief systems and their religious practices. They began to pray together. And they began to cross church thresholds to hear preaching, sing in choirs, and marry people of other religious backgrounds. At the level of official church life, formal and enduring dialogues were supported. One such dialogue was the Roman Catholic and the Presbyterian/Reformed Consultation, and one of the topics was "Laity in the Church and in the World." As a participant in this dialogue, I experienced how the intellectual search for understanding, shared prayer, and shared life can reveal the common ground that sustains us all.

Dialoguing with these ecumenical partners sharpened my own understanding of terms and concepts and spiritual realities that centered my life. At one point we agreed that "the partners are not 'converted' to each other's views. Rather, the uniqueness of each other is expanded even as the sharing of life and faith experiences grows between them. The dialogue and the encounters are a means of spiritual formation of the participants...."[27]

IMPLEMENTATION OF THE
DECLARATION ON CHRISTIAN EDUCATION

The themes of *Gravissimum Educationis* moved forward with dispatch in many parts of the world, and in the United States with notable energy. One point of affirmation in the document concerns the value of interdisciplinary (liberal arts) education. That, together with *Apostolicam Actuositatem*'s promotion of the role of the laity within society and the church, helped move Catholic colleges and universities in a new direction.

Higher Education

Many believe the decisive change in higher education occurring in the years immediately following the close of the council, was the laicization of boards of trustees. The effect of adding laity to these boards (of more than three hundred colleges and universities) was to shift the authority of governance from religious orders, who had founded these institutions and sustained them for decades, to boards of laity and religious, thereby putting into meaningful practice the principle of shared responsibility for the mission of the church.

There were many reasons for this substantial change, including college presidents' realization that governance of religious communities and governance in education were best attended to separately. According to Alice Gallin, OSU, who has written a definitive study of the change in governance, Catholic educators looked to the council for the theological and pastoral undergirding for the changes they were proposing. "The documents of Vatican II were just being disseminated, and the ecclesial encouragement to increasing the role and responsibility of the laity in church institutions was the perfect complement to many other reasons expressed by the presidents."[28]

The change did not happen without debate and doubts. Would there be competent laity to fill these important positions? How would the unique charisms of the founding religious orders be preserved under lay governance? Would laicization inevitably lead to secularization? What defines a Catholic college or university? These questions were at the center of the discussions between bishops and college/university presidents occasioned by the promulgation of the apostolic constitution *Ex Corde Ecclesiae* in 1990. They continued for a decade, resulting in "The Application of *Ex corde Ecclesiae* for the United States," which states its preference for a majority of trustees to be committed Catholics. But the addition of the phrase, "to the extent possible" left institutional leadership with room to make prudential judgments in the matter.[29]

The discussions engendered by *Ex Corde* were intense, candid, and ultimately judged as possibly "a graced moment."[30] Implied in the notion of a "graced moment" is that continuing conversation about identity, faith, culture, pastoral outreach, and the relationship of higher education to the civil community and to the universal and local church is a good thing. As a result, many institutions are more committed to clarity about Catholic identity. Jesuit colleges and universities, for example, now typically have in place a person responsible for maintaining Catholic *and* Jesuit identity.

One continuing point of tension is around the *mandatum*, applicable to theologians. This is an acknowledgment by local, competent church authority that a Catholic professor of a theological discipline is a teacher in full communion with the Catholic Church. In most educational institutions individual professors of theology seek the *mandatum* from the local bishop on their own initiative. It is, in fact, a private matter between them.

One place where *Apostolicam Actuositatem* and *Gravissimum Educationis* converge is the importance of educating laity for responsibility in the social arena. Several years ago I interviewed some students from several different colleges and asked the question: What would you tell college presidents is needed to educate laity for good citizenship in the public square? Their responses were as follows:

1. Education for social justice is important, but as long as it's totally abstract it's ineffective. Liberal arts colleges can and should provide experiences for students.

2. Isolated concrete experiences are not sufficient. Two weeks in Appalachia or a semester in Jerusalem will not be sufficiently formative. A center of some kind is needed where the conversation of the learning community is intentionally focused on life in the public square.

3. Providing an international perspective is critical. We live in a world of permeable borders, a world where strangers quickly become our neighbor, and ongoing dialogue about this reality is needed.

These students seemed to have absorbed the teaching of Vatican II about the connection between education and increased awareness of the laity's role in creating a more just society. Furthermore, a number of universities and colleges, do in fact, have centers whose purpose is the type of experienced-based social justice education highlighted in these interviews. This is a tribute to the vision and leadership of college presidents and faculty and to the students whom these leaders empower.[31]

To Teach as Jesus Did (1972)

This pastoral message on Catholic education was one of the first steps in implementing the council's teaching on education and the laity. It starts by saying, "The pastoral is...written against the background of the Second Vatican Council's *Declaration on Christian Education* which requested national hierarchies to issue detailed statements on the educational ministry considered in the context of the Church and society in their own countries."[32] While technically this is a statement of the bishops and represents their views on the state of education at that time, it was crafted in a consultative way. In fact, the statement is clear that the text is the result of wide consultation, inclusive of a variety of backgrounds. Like *Called and Gifted*, which was approved a few years later, *To Teach as Jesus Did* declares that the pastoral is not the "final word."

Rather it is "a catalyst to help people deal with the problems of polarization and confusion now confronting the educational ministry."[33]

To Teach as Jesus Did faithfully reflects *Gravissimum Educationis* and its context of community, communication, justice, and service. Adult education is highlighted with a strong affirmation of the benefits of life-long learning. It is also recognized as a *mutual* enterprise between instructors and learners. In this, the document is in harmony with the best of adult education principles and methodology. All aspects of life are touched by the commitment to adult education: family life including parent education; education in social justice; and the preparation of parents to be the first educators on human sexuality for their children.

Higher education is dealt with, particularly regarding the importance of campus ministry at secular institutions (*GE*, 10). And, anticipating the concerns of *Ex Corde Ecclesiae*, the document promotes continuing dialogue between colleges/universities and church authorities.[34]

The always contentious issue of sex education is faced clearly in *To Teach as Jesus Did*. The bishops had already affirmed, in 1968, the value of education in human sexuality (*Human Life in Our Time*), saying that the church has a grave obligation to assist parents in educating their children in these matters. *To Teach as Jesus Did* takes the issue a step further by saying that parents should not transfer their own anxiety about the subject to indiscriminate opposition to school instruction in human sexuality. The bishops stress that responsible classroom instruction includes the spiritual and moral aspects of sexuality. Despite reliance on *Gravissimum Educationis* and the positive experiences of many dioceses in the area of education in human sexuality, the issue of classroom instruction continues to provoke activist opposition by some parents, and it may also be a factor in the growth of home schooling in Catholic families.[35]

THE NEXUS OF LAY MINISTRY AND CHRISTIAN EDUCATION

During the post-council years, much of the history of the growth of lay leadership in the church has been intertwined with Christian education. In addition to their involvement in the governance of institutions of higher education, the laity's role in America's Catholic school systems and in religious education, in particular, continues to be an expansive and expanding one. Most of the teachers and administrators of Catholic schools are now lay. Most of the catechetical instructors are lay. Principals and superintendents of schools are lay. A torch has, indeed, passed. Furthermore, according to one prominent canon lawyer, the question of whether bishops may designate laity to share in juridic authority has been answered. How? Lay principals are regularly designated to act "*in locus episcopus*"—a juridical act.[36]

It would seem that now, in the first years of the third millennium, the table is set for laity to participate ever more fully in the fellowship and mission of the church. Perhaps, but the state of the questions is far from settled.

PART IV

THE STATE OF THE QUESTIONS

THE DECREE ON THE APOSTOLATE OF THE LAITY
APOSTOLICAM ACTUOSITATEM

The Second Vatican Council's emphasis on the laity had the effect of repositioning the laity's place in the church. Forty years ago, the laity began to move from the narthex to the nave, and then into the sanctuary. There, in both nave and sanctuary, the laity have been active participants in worship, management, and outreach of all kinds. They are, in fact, considered ministers, certainly in terms of their own self-identity. But fellow laity who benefit from their service also regard them as such, as do deacons, priests, and bishops who know and trust their competence and dedication. Experiments in shared responsibility (with pastoral councils and lay ecclesial ministry) have, over the years, been successful. Stories of these experiments are related in Part Three.

Yet the metaphor I would use to describe the place of the laity at this time is *standing at the threshold*. Why? The clergy sex abuse scandal in the United States has affected the laity as no other issue in recent history. When the scandals became public, laity everywhere—in the narthex, the nave, the sanctuary, and beyond the church doors—were stunned. Why did their leaders whom they loved and respected act so ineptly? Why were good priests, outside the circle of scandal, conflated with the perpetrators? Laity saw their church's credibility and financial stability disappear. They were angry and sorrowful and they began to gather around the church's threshold at the point between church and society, the threshold being the strongest part of any structure. It's where one goes during an earthquake. And the scandals have surely been an ecclesial earthquake.

As for the official leaders at the national level—bishops in particular —many believe they are reluctant to press forward with the vision of the council. Energy and imagination appear to have been redirected into a survival mode. Clearly, lawsuits and bankruptcies have drained financial and human resources. Bluntly stated: there are few funds available for the continuing education and formation of the laity as called for by the council and by popes and by bishops.

Furthermore, bishops who had been present at the council—or personally influenced by it in some way—are now either retired or dead. (It is estimated that only eight "council" bishops worldwide are still living.) In the face of all this, where can we hope to continue *Apostolicam Actuositatem*'s agenda of lay participation and leadership in the church of today? Once again, let us look to the thresholds.

New Lay Organizations

A number of post-council lay organizations were discussed in Part Three. Two new ones, however, are the result of this twenty-first-century church crisis. The first, comprised of committed, experienced, and astute laity, The Church in America: The Leadership Roundtable, stands at the threshold of business and church. The organization had its beginnings in 2003 with concerned business leaders wondering how they could help the Catholic Church manage better. Since then, there have been two national gatherings of leaders from the non-profit, profit, and religious worlds. The intent was and is to offer to the church the best practices of business, which can help assure accountability in church matters. The business leaders are renowned in their own circles. They are skilled at both making money and raising money. Furthermore, their spirituality tends to place these skills in the context of stewardship. Therefore, they are willing to share their knowledge with church leaders at all levels.

Will the bishops be willing and able to use this offer of giftedness? That remains an open question. While *Apostolicam Actuositatem* states that laity may utilize their own unique experience in assuming responsibility for their organization (*AA*, 20) and praises groups most responsive "to the needs of time and place" (*AA*, 21), pastors are ultimately responsible for the church. The essential ingredient in this mix is trust, and the building of trust may take a great deal of perseverance and patience and willingness, the opposite of willfulness.[1]

The second organization is the Voice of the Faithful. It began in a Boston parish where laity and their pastor *together* reflected on how to salvage the church's credibility in the archdiocese of Boston, the epicenter of the crisis. Before long, others in the archdiocese joined them, and soon the organization spread throughout the nation.

Reflecting the Decree on the Apostolate of the Laity, this new organization's mission is clear and unambiguous. It states its love for the church, its commitment to renewal, its recognition of the hierarchical ordering of the church, and its support for victims of clergy sexual abuse and for faithful priests. The organization holds an annual meeting and now has an affiliate structure; that is, parishes and universities can belong (and they do) and receive materials that highlight the teachings of *Apostolicam Actuositatem* and of canon law. In fact, the noted canon lawyer Ladislas Orsy, SJ, is a consultant to the group. The Voice of the Faithful is engaged in educational efforts for *all the laity*, hoping to revive energy for the reforms enacted by the council.[2]

Both of these new organizations are clear in stating that their focus is not on what might be called "neuralgic issues," such as optional celibacy, ordination of women, and reproductive questions. Their purposes are clearly defined and aligned with *Apostolicam Actuositatem*. Yet some bishops are suspicious of the organizations. A challenge, then, is how to promote dialogue between these "awakened" laity and their bishops. An open-minded, open-hearted study of Pope Paul VI's first encyclical, *Ecclesiam Suam*, might be instructive to all. There the pope speaks of dialogue as spiritual communication marked by:

- clear, understandable language

- meekness, a virtue that makes our dialogue peaceful and patient

- trust between speaker and the listener

- sensitivity to the situation and needs of the hearer.[3]

Granted, Paul VI wrote these words in reference to ecumenical dialogue, but over the years this wisdom has been applied to all kinds of dialogue. Indeed, if the above characteristics can help ecumenical and inter-faith conversation, why not the *conversatio* so needed for conversion of those within the same communion?

Lay Ecclesial Ministry

The threshold is also an entrance. And in the past quarter of a century, laity (a large proportion of them women) have professionally prepared for lay ministry within the church, at all levels (see Part Three). It is reasonable to assume that in the years to come these new ministers will assume more responsibility for parish life and for diocesan leadership. The shift is a result of two factors: a shortage of priests and the development of the theology of baptism. The presence of the laity introduces a new context as they pursue studies while still inserted in their homes (the domestic church) and serving as responsible citizens of their larger communities. One could say they consciously live in two worlds, neither of which is like the seminary culture, although their theological training is rigorous. Lay ecclesial ministers can, and I believe will, have the effect of changing what has been called "the clerical culture" (during the council debates referred to as "clericalism") as more and more of them (especially women) cross the threshold. Still, there are some clergy, mostly bishops, who continue to question the appropriateness of the "ministry terminology" for laity.

When the landmark document *Co-workers in the Vineyard of the Lord* was approved by the USCCB in November 2005, objections were raised about the language. *Co-workers* is described as a "Resource for Guiding the Development of Lay Ecclesial Ministry." It is not intended to set down norms, but rather to relate the history of lay ecclesial ministry, models of training, the theological undergirding of the phenomenon—in other words, it is meant as a resource for bishops *who wish to use it*. Still, some bishops spoke (or wrote) that while *ministry* might be acceptable, the word "minister" as applied to laity was not. Implicit in this reasoning seems to be the question of whether the use of "minister" in reference to laity might confuse the distinction between the ordained and the lay minister.

The 1997 Roman document, "Instruction on Certain Questions Regarding the Collaboration of the Non-Ordained Faithful in the

Sacramental Ministry of Priests" was invoked by some as a warning that merited extreme caution. This despite the fact that at the time of its issuance (early November 1997) Bishop James Hoffman of Toledo, a canon lawyer and a member of the sub-committee on Lay Ecclesial Ministry, went to Rome on behalf of the bishops' conference to receive the document. He reported to the general assembly that, based on the exchange of views at the Vatican meeting and his own reading of it, the *Instruction* is intended for countries where problems exist regarding *roles*. The United States, he said, was *not* in a state of confusion; the work of the conference had been helpful to individual bishops and would continue to be.[4]

During the debate on *Co-workers in the Vineyard*, Cardinal Avery Dulles, generally considered a conservative theologian, vigorously defended the use of the terms "lay minister" and "lay ministry."

The document is clearly needed. According to recent statistics, there were (in 2005) 30,632 lay ecclesial ministers working at least twenty hours a week in paid positions in U.S. Catholic parishes and 2,163 doing such work at least twenty hours a week on a volunteer basis. The paid ecclesial ministers, as of 2005, outnumbered priests engaged in parish ministry. More than 40 percent of lay ecclesial ministers are directors of religious education, and one-fourth are general pastoral associates. Others are youth ministers, music ministers, or engaged in liturgy and planning.[5]

Religious and Laity Together

According to Webster's dictionary, the threshold is that point at which psychological change takes place. And spiritual change occurs there too. This kind of threshold is now under construction in many religious communities of vowed women religious. For example, the Sisters of Mercy of the Americas have lay associates who are involved in Mercy missions and who experience a form of Mercy formation. The same is true of many other religious orders of women.

Vowed men religious are also more intentionally aligned with the laity. While the Benedictines have long had Oblates (i.e., lay people educated in the Rule of Benedict at a particular monastery and attached to that monastery) associated with them, a few Cistercian (Trappist) monasteries have recently undertaken similar formation programs for laity. This opens up a new horizon for this cloistered order.

The Society of Jesus now has a major commitment to include laity, and in particular women, in its various missions. The 34th General Congregation of the Jesuits in 1995 set this in motion. The Maryland Jesuit Province is responding by offering common continuing spiritual formation for Jesuits and their lay collaborators. Since the council, the Ignatian Spiritual Exercises have been enriching lay life in numerous ways; lay participants not only receive spiritual direction, they *are* directors. Consequently, they are now in positions of spiritual leadership in Jesuit missions, responsible for priests as well as laity. Their numbers are likely to increase as numbers of available Jesuits for leadership decrease. What is notable, however, is that the change is not happening in a haphazard way. The ground is being cultivated so that the ordained and lay leaders are together placing themselves before the Spirit of God, open, available to, and accountable to one another in the spirit of true companionship.

All of these examples illustrate how new alliances of religious and laity are currently being forged. As the future unfolds, these new designs are where we should look to discern the action of the Spirit in the third millennium. They exist not only for the renewal of religious orders but also for the renewal of the church and, ultimately, of society.

Theology from Below

The lay initiatives regarding church accountability, the growth of lay ecclesial ministry at all levels of the church, and the intentional association of laypeople with religious communities in spiritual formation and the enactment of their missions are where we should look for the continuing implementation of the council's teaching on the indispensable role of the laity. These are hope-filled developments, situated within the traditions of the church. Qualities of authentic leadership—collaboration, courage, creativity, commitment, and compassion—are evident in all these undertakings. These qualities have also been seen in certain educational sites.

THE DECLARATION ON CHRISTIAN EDUCATION
GRAVISSIMUM EDUCATIONIS

The state of Catholic education today is mixed. There is a sense that the years immediately following the council led to a weakening in the teaching of doctrine. In addition, the "Catholic culture" that emanated from Catholic schools underwent a change. Some said that culture was becoming barely recognizable. These and other factors led to the publication of the *Catechism of the Catholic Church* in 1994, an effort to inform and clarify. Also, curricula, which in some cases was deemed "thin," has thickened considerably.

In the early post-council years a number of Catholic schools closed. More recently, new schools have been opening, largely because of parents who are willing to pay for them. These schools are now staffed and administered largely by laypeople, and so require a more substantial budget than in earlier times when religious were essentially volunteers.

The situation in inner cities, however, is different. There, not only are schools being closed, but so are the sponsoring parishes. This has caused a great deal of anguish to people and priests. Although dioceses have traditionally underwritten the costs of the urban schools where much of the student population is non-Catholic, today some dioceses are facing lawsuits that are draining diocesan budgets. Still, here and there, diocesan sacrificial efforts continue to provide for what amounts to an alternative school system for poor inner city children.

Both the Declaration on Christian Education and *To Teach as Jesus Did* opened the door to sex education in the schools, all the while recognizing that parents are the primary educators of their children. Nevertheless, the issue of sex education programs in Catholic schools (and in public schools for that matter) has never been resolved to everyone's satisfaction. Again, the recent scandals have had an influence. The USCCB now requires that every school have a child protection program that teaches children how to recognize and react to inappropriate adult behavior. Even in this new climate, there remain pockets of parental disapproval of such mandated school programs.[6]

Social Justice Education

One of the continuing success stories is education for social justice. This education begins early on, and continues through adult programs. Justice and peace networks have been especially helpful in keeping Catholic social teaching in the center of educational priorities.

The notion of the "seamless garment" proposed by Cardinal Joseph Bernardin has been a way of drawing attention to the many places of church concern. One last threshold, however, is that of capital punishment. The USCCB has recently initiated a program to urge the nation to rethink the premises of this practice. But questions remain: Will the pro-life movement embrace this issue as it has other end-of-life issues? Will capital punishment be consistently inserted in the social action agenda? Will there be adequate education about this complex question in school curricula as well as in adult education programs? These are becoming more pressing questions deserving of the church's attention.

Catholic Higher Education

Catholic higher education continues to be laicized (not secularized), with continuing concern about maintaining the unique charisms of the religious founders of the institutions. As more Catholic colleges are led by *lay* presidents, the challenges for identifying the unique identity of each college will be more pronounced. Tensions regarding the *mandatum* seem to be waning, as each bishop handles the issue and its consequences according to the local situation. The way the issue is being addressed is a vivid example of the wisdom of subsidiarity. The differentiation between Catholicism and catholicity may prove to be a way to deeper understanding of the state of *this* question.[7]

New Initiatives

Two higher education initiatives occasioned by the sexual abuse scandal in Boston have created venues for sustained study and reflection on various dimensions of contemporary church life. One is located at Saint Thomas More Chapel at Yale University.

The chapel had long maintained a serious lecture program, bringing distinguished Catholic speakers to examine topics of the day from a faith perspective. In late spring of 2002, the chapel's board of trustees reflected on how best to address the revelations of clergy sexual abuse. They thought the situation warranted a large undertaking, large in breadth and depth. They concluded that the underlying problem of the crisis was that of the exercise of governance and leadership. A conference on "Governance, Accountability and the Future of the Church" was held at Yale in March 2002. An international gathering of bishops, priests, women religious, and laity came together for the event. "Although the scandals surrounding the issue of sexual abuse had provided the impetus for the conference, its purpose was neither to focus on those scandals as such, nor to criticize particular individuals."[8] The focus was on deeper questions regarding *how* the crisis could have occurred the way it did. The conference examined theological and canonical perspectives, legal, political, and financial aspects and the challenges and opportunities in the American church. An important book based on the prepared papers has been published and is listed in Part Five. Whether or not the Yale Catholic chapel will follow up on the conference and its publication is not clear. It may be that the Yale Catholic leaders will find ways to collaborate with the second higher education project, The Church of the 21st Century.

The Church of the 21st Century, located at Boston College, originated in September of 2002. Intended to be a two-year project to explore the problematic issues highlighted by the sexual abuse scandal, it continues to study those issues. The Church of the 21st Century now sees its role as one of movement from crisis to renewal with three major areas of concern:

1. sharing the faith with the next generation

2. understanding the roles of laymen and laywomen, vowed religious, priests, and bishops

3. reflection on sexuality in the Catholic tradition and contemporary culture

This ongoing program sponsors conferences and lectures and has a publication, *C21 Resources*, and a web site. In 2005, The Church of the 21st
Century received the Cardinal Bernardin Catholic Common Ground
award.

Adult Education

The adult education so emphasized by *Gravissimum Educationis* has
perdured in the Catholic community and has been declared a priority
by the bishops (following numerous statements by Pope John Paul II).
More than twenty-five years after *To Teach as Jesus Did*, a pastoral plan
devoted solely to adult faith formation was approved by the entire
body of bishops. *Our Hearts Were Burning Within Us* placed adult education (faith formation) squarely at the center of the church's educational ministry, a sign that this priority of *Gravissimum Educationis* has
not been forgotten.

The pastoral plan is in a line of earlier projects. Youth ministry and
catechesis were addressed in *Renewing the Vision; Sons and Daughters of
the Light* was a pastoral plan for young adults. But *Our Hearts Were
Burning Within Us* pulls together the threads of *how* to make the lay
apostolate live. So, one could say it takes the message of both *Apostolicam Actuositatem* and *Gravissimum Educationis* to the realm of the practical or the doable, all the while keeping the vision of the Emmaus story
sharp and crisp. It is an integrating document, a plan for the long haul.
It hopes to ignite a passion for renewal of adult faith formation.

At the same time, it is no "pie in the sky" statement. The challenges and concerns of contemporary life are noted. What is *not* there,
in this 1999 document, is the trauma of the abuse scandal. What *is*
there is the conviction that a living faith is possible and that it can be
nourished. "A living faith is keenly conscious and aware of the power
and hold of sin in human life (cf. Heb. 12:1, Rom. 7:14-25). Like the
Church, the person of mature faith is 'at once holy and always in need
of purification'" (*LG*, 8).[9] This approach can be enormously consoling
in times of confusion and anger, times like our own.

The document sets forth goals, principles, and dimensions of faith
formation (from doctrine to liturgy to moral formation to the inner

life of prayer). It has sound suggestions about and for leadership. Indeed, as laity and pastors strive for some way to recover their balance and their trust, the path of adult education in its many forms can be a path of hope. Laywomen and laymen need to know the current foundational, reliable teachings about their church, and their role in it. They need to know the documents of the Second Vatican Council, the highest level of teaching authority in the Roman Catholic Church in our time, and to discover therein their rights, their responsibilities, their roles as articulated in this great ecclesial event of the twentieth century.

I started this section of the book by suggesting that a metaphor for the laity in these times is "standing at the threshold." A well informed, prayerful, humble, and courageous laity have the potential of making the threshold a place of welcome and dynamism.

Who will separate us from the love of Christ? asks the apostle Paul. And he answers, "I am convinced that neither death, nor life, nor angels, nor rulers, nor things present, nor things to come, nor powers, nor height, nor depth, nor anything else in all creation, will be able to separate us from the love of God in Christ Jesus our Lord" (Rom 8:38–39).

That is our heritage.

NOTES

PART I: THE DOCUMENTS

1. Quoted by Paul Lakeland in *The Liberation of the Laity: In Search of an Accountable Church* (New York: Continuum, 2003), 17.

2. Ibid., chapter 2.

3. Father Congar mentioned this fear at the Vienna Meeting; see also Lakeland, *The Liberation of the Laity*, 51.

4. Bernard Lonergan's theological method stresses a number of particular steps in decision-making. These include *being attentive to data, being intelligent (i.e., exploring), being reasonable (i.e., discerning), and being responsible.* See *Spiritual Exercises for Church Leaders* by Dolores Leckey and Paula Minaert (Paulist Press, 2003).

5. See H. Richard McCord, "Full, Conscious, and Active Participation: The Laity's Quest," in *Vatican II, The Continuing Agenda: Lay People in the Church and in Society*, ed. Anthony J. Cernera (Fairfield, CT: Sacred Heart Press, 1997).

6. Rosemary Goldie, *From a Roman Window* (Australia: HarperCollins Religious, 1998), 6.

7. Ibid., 16.

8. Ibid., 20.

9. Ibid., 37.

10. Gail Porter Mandell, *Madeleva: One Woman's Life* (New York/Mahwah, NJ: Paulist Press, 1994), 41.

11. Sister Madeleva, *My First Seventy Years* (New York: Macmillan, 1959), 3; cited by Mandell in *Madeleva*, 43.

12. Mandell, *Madeleva*, 43.

13. Goldie, *From a Roman Window*, 70.

14. Ibid., 70–71.

15. Xavier Rynne, "The Third Session: The Debates and Decrees of Vatican Council II, September 14 to November 21, 1964," in *Vatican Council II* (New York: Farrar, Straus and Giroux, 1968), 83.

16. See Leon-Joseph Suenens, *The Hidden Hand of God* (Dublin: Veritas Publications, 1994).

17. Rynne, "The Third Session," 65.

18. Ibid., 69.

19. Ibid.

20. Ibid.

21. Ibid., 70.

22. For details of this segment of the debate, see Rynne, "The Third Session," 70–73.

23. Rynne, "The Third Session," 73–74.

24. See *Origins*, Catholic News Service, October 1987, for interventions at the synod on the laity.

25. Suenens, *The Hidden Hand of God*.

26. Rynne, "The Third Session," 71.

27. Ibid., 72.

28. Ibid., 82.

PART II: MAJOR POINTS

1. *Co-Workers in the Vineyard of the Lord: A Resource for Guiding the Development of Lay Ecclesial Ministry*," United States Conference of Catholic Bishops (USCCB), 2005.

2. See *Follow the Way of Love* for a treatment of the domestic church. USCCB, 1994.

3. The notion of a mandate appears decades later in the United States in reference to higher education in *Ex Corde Ecclesiae* (specifically with regard to teachers of theology receiving a *mandate* from the local bishop to teach Catholic theology).

4. *Strengthening the Bonds of Peace*, USCCB, 1994.

5. Bernard Lonergan, *Method in Theology* (Toronto: University of Toronto Press, 1990, 1994, and 1996).

PART III: IMPLEMENTATION

1. Rosemary Goldie, *From a Roman Window* (Australia: HarperCollins Religious, 1998), 143.

2. Ibid.

3. The U.S. bishops have since reorganized into one conference: The United States Conference of Catholic Bishops (USCCB).

4. I have this attribution in my notes from one of the Woodstock "Ignatius-Lonergan" seminars in which Woodstock fellows participate twice a month.

5. The details of the Call to Action project (consultation and Detroit conference) were obtained from author interviews with Archbishop (Emeritus) Peter Leo Gerety, Bishop James Malone (Youngstown), Bishop Thomas Gumbleton (Detroit), Dr. Francis J. Butler, president of FADICA (Founders and Donors Interested in Catholic Activities), Jerry Filteau of Catholic News Service, Walter Grazer of the USCCB Dept. of International Justice and Peace, Timothy Collins, deputy director of the CCHD, and from Pope Paul VI's address, which can be found in the USCCB archives.

6. David O'Brien, *The National Catholic Reporter*, February 25, 1977.

7. USCCB archives, "Call to Action" files.

8. See Dolores Leckey, "Response" to Scott Appleby's 2000 Catholic Common Ground Lecture, *The Substance of Things Hoped For*, available from the National Pastoral Life Center in New York City.

9. *Called and Gifted*, p. 4.

10. Ibid., p. 7.

11. Ibid., p. 8.

12. Ibid., p. 9.

13. Ibid., p. 8.

14. Ibid., p. 2.

15. Paul Lakeland, *The Liberation of the Laity: In Search of an Accountable Church* (New York: Continuum, 2003), 132.

16. *Called and Gifted for the Third Millennium*, p. 17.

17. Ibid., p. 15.

18. See Roger Cardinal Mahony and the Priests of Los Angeles, *As I Have Done For You: A Pastoral Letter on Ministry*, April 20, 2000.

19. These synod observations are taken from the author's notes on the 1987 synod, at which she was present.

20. The narrative concerning developments in the Bishops' Committee on Women (including the pastoral letter) is based on materials in the USCCB archives and author interviews with Bishops McAuliffe and Imesch. Portions of it appeared in *CHURCH*, Winter, 2001.

21. The taxonomy of these three feminist positions is from an unpublished paper presented by Sandra Schneiders, IHM, at an invitational symposium sponsored by the Bishops' Committee on Women in 1995.

22. Catherine Mowry LaCugna, "Catholic Women as Ministers and Theologians," *America*, October 10, 1992.

23. Survey data available from the USCCB Secretariat for Family, Laity, Women and Youth in Washington, DC.

24. *Co-Workers in the Vineyard of the Lord: A Resource for Guiding the Development of Lay Ecclesial Ministry* was approved by the bishops at their November 2005 plenary session.

25. See Roger Cardinal Mahony, "As One Who Serves" and "Lay Leadership for Parishes." Both documents can be found in *Origins*, October 13, 2005. See also "Working Together in Preparation for Service: Collaboration as a Hallmark of Formation for Ministry," a statement of the St. Francis Seminary faculty, Archdiocese of Milwaukee.

26. This description of the San Egidio community is from *Spiritual Exercises for Church Leaders* by Dolores Leckey and Paula Minaert (New York/ Mahwah, NJ: Paulist Press, 2003).

27. *Laity in the Church and in the World, Roman Catholic and Reformed Church Consultation*, USCCB, 1998.

28. Alice Gallin, *Independence and a New Partnership in Catholic Higher Education* (South Bend, IN: University of Notre Dame Press, 1996).

29. *The Application of* Ex corde Ecclesiae *for the United States*, (Washington, DC: USCCB Publications Dept., 2000).

30. Ibid., p. 7.

31. The University of Notre Dame and Georgetown University are two institutions with such centers; there are, of course, others.

32. *To Teach as Jesus Did*, USCCB, 1972, p. 1.

33. Ibid., p. 2.

34. Ibid., p. 21.

35. In an attempt to address the tensions around sex education in Catholic Schools, the U.S. bishops issued a number of statements, including *Human Sexuality: A Catholic Perspective for Education and Lifelong Learning*, USCCB Publishing, 1991.

36. John P. Beal, *The Jurist* 55 (1995): 1, p. 91. "The Exercise of the Power of Governance by Lay People: State of the Question."

PART IV: THE STATE OF THE QUESTIONS

1. The Church in America Leadership Roundtable is currently "housed" at the Office of FADICA (Founders and Donors Interested in Catholic Activities). Ms. Kerry Robinson is the founding executive director.

2. The Voice of the Faithful has an extensive website replete with the history of the organization, its many projects, and essays relevant to its mission.

3. Pope Paul VI, encyclical *Ecclesiam Suam* (Paths of the Church), 81.

4. *Co-workers in the Vineyard of the Lord: A Resource for Guiding the Development of Lay Ecclesial Ministry* is available from USCCB Publishing. It is also on the USCCB website. This document is the result of ten years of research, theological reflection, and participation by a wide spectrum of bishops.

5. See Catholic News Service article by Jerry Filteau, November 16, 2005.

6. USCCB Publishing lists a number of resources relevant to the sexual abuse crisis.

7. The Woodstock Theological Center has a project now in progress that addresses the differentiation between catholicity, understood to be a movement toward wholeness and Catholicism, the institutional handing on of the Catholic faith. Father John Haughey, SJ, is directing this project.

8. Francis Oakley and Bruce Russett, eds., *Governance, Accountability, and the Future of the Catholic Church* (New York: Continuum International Publishing Group, 2004), 7.

9. *Our Hearts Were Burning Within Us*, USCCB Publishing, 1999, p. 17.

PART V
FURTHER READING

RESOURCES RELEVANT TO PARTS I AND II—
BEFORE AND DURING THE COUNCIL

Walter M. Abbot, SJ, general editor. *The Documents of Vatican II*. New York: Herder & Herder, 1966. This is the translation/version that has probably been most widely used during the past forty years. However, in this book I used the Vatican's translation, available from that website.

Yves Congar, OP. *Lay People in the Church: A Study for a Theology of the Laity*. Westminster, MD: Newman, 1955; rev. ed. 1965. A major source for understanding the theological assumptions and reasoning that helped shape the Decree on the Apostolate of the Laity.

Rosemary Goldie. *From a Roman Window: Five Decades—The World, The Church and the Catholic Laity*. Australia: HarperCollins Religious, 1998. A first-hand account of the forces behind the laity movement prior to and during the council as well as the years of implementation, told by the first woman to work in the Vatican curia.

Paul Lakeland. *The Liberation of the Laity: In Search of an Accountable Church*. New York: Continuum, 2003. The early chapters are a helpful review of the theologians who, in the decades before the council, concentrated on the essential role of the laity in the church. The book also includes an interesting discussion of secularity and the spirituality associated with it.

Gail Porter Mandell. *Madeleva, A Biography*. Albany: State University of New York Press, 1997. This biography of the long-serving president of Saint Mary's College in South Bend, Indiana, is insightful regarding the pathways of intellectual excellence and autonomy forged in the Catholic higher education in the years prior to the council. An early indicator of alliances between laity (especially laywomen) and vowed religious.

Kenan B. Osborne, OFM. *Ministry: Lay Ministry in the Roman Catholic Church*. New York/Mahwah, NJ: Paulist Press, 1993. The first five hundred pages of this magisterially sweeping view of the place of the layperson in the church take the reader through all the periods of Christian history: from the first century and the meaning of discipleship to the patristic period, to the Middle Ages, to the Reformation, to Trent, and up to Second Vatican Council.

Xavier Rynne (pseudonym for Redemptorist Father Francis Xavier Murphy). *Vatican Council II*. New York: Farrar, Straus and Giroux, 1968. A description, in great detail, of the public (and sometimes private) debates about the drafts of various documents. Written in a highly accessible, journalistic style, the section on session three will be of particular interest to readers of this book. It was during that session that the fate of the documents on the laity and on Christian education hung in the balance.

Leon-Joseph Suenens. *Memories and Hopes*. Dublin: Veritas Publications, 1991. Cardinal Suenens, one of the four moderators of the council, relates his own remembrances and experiences "from the inside." The book is also a tribute to his deep personal friendship with Pope John XXIII.

RESOURCES RELEVANT TO PARTS III AND IV—
AFTER THE COUNCIL

Laity and Lay Ministry

Available from USCCB Publishing:

Called and Gifted, Reflections on American Catholic Laity (1980). This was the first official statement by an episcopal conference after the promulgation of the Decree on the Apostolate of the Laity. It has been called a blueprint for ensuing statements.

Called and Gifted for the Third Millennium (1995). An updated and expanded version of the first *Called and Gifted*.

Strengthening the Bonds of Peace (1994). While the focus of this statement is the value of women's leadership and giftedness for the life of the church, much is applicable to men, and thus to all laity.

From Words to Deeds, Continuing Reflections on the Role of Women in the Church (1998). Produced by the Committee on Women in Society and in the Church, this statement is intended to offer encouragement to all church leaders, lay, ordained, and religious, to put into practice recent teachings regarding the equality of women, their gifts, and their valued leadership.

Together in God's Service: Toward a Theology of Ecclesial Lay Ministry, Papers from a Colloquium (1998). The papers in this small volume probe the theological and pastoral developments in lay ministry. The colloquium brought together theologians and bishops.

Lay Ecclesial Ministry: The State of the Questions (1999). Discusses the current term, "lay ecclesial minister," the preparation of lay ecclesial ministers, the relationship between lay ecclesial ministers and ordained ministers, and other important questions.

Co-Workers in the Vineyard of the Lord: A Resource for Guiding the Development of Lay Ecclesial Ministry" (2005). Examines theological foundations, discernment, and suitability for lay ecclesial ministry; formation and authorization of lay ecclesial ministers; and policies and practices in the ministerial workplace.

Papal Statements:

John Paul II, *Christifideles Laici* (1988). The apostolic exhortation on the Christian lay faithful, written after the 1987 synod on the "Vocation and Mission of the Laity in the Church and in the World."

————. *Mulieris Dignitatem* (1988). This apostolic letter, referred to by the pope as a meditation on women, endorses equality and participation of women in church life.

————. *The Genius of Women.* This compilation of papal statements prior to the U.N. Conference on Women in 1995 provides insights into the pope's claim to be a "feminist."

Other Publications:

Zeni Fox. *New Ecclesial Ministry: Lay Professionals Serving the Church.* Revised and expanded edition. Maryland: Rowman and Littlefield, 2002. A non-ideological and thorough review of the development of lay ministry in our time. The book is timely and credible.

Zeni Fox and Regina Bechtle, SC. *Called and Chosen: Toward a Spirituality for Lay Leaders.* Maryland: Rowman and Littlefield, 2005. Provides broad and deep views of lay leaders in many different roles: their sense of vocation, their institutional missions, their inner lives.

Edward P. Hahnenberg. *Ministries: A Relational Approach*. New York: Cross-road, 2003. The author places relationships at the heart of all ministry.

Dolores R. Leckey. *Laity Stirring the Church, Prophetic Questions*. Philadel-phia: Fortress Press, 1987. Considers the ways in which laity act as catalysts for change: in the workplace, in their families, in defining community, and in ministry.

Paul J. Philibert, OP. *The Priesthood of the Faithful: Key to a Living Church*. Collegeville, MN: Liturgical Press, 2005. A study of baptism and its implica-tions for a revitalized laity and a revitalized church.

Christian Education

Available from USCCB Publishing:

To Teach as Jesus Did (1972). Like *Called and Gifted*, this document is consid-ered a blueprint for subsequent laity statements. *To Teach as Jesus Did* deals with the continuing implementation of the Declaration on Christian Educa-tion. See Part Three for a discussion of this document.

Ex Corde Ecclesiae (1990). This apostolic constitution on higher education has to do with the identity and mission of Catholic universities and contains general norms to be applied at the local and regional levels by episcopal conferences.

The Application of Ex corde Ecclesiae for the United States. This document was approved in 1999 by the Plenary Assembly of the National Conference of Catholic Bishops (now the USCCB). It has the force of particular law for the United States.

Guidelines Concerning the Academic Mandatum in Catholic Universities (2001). These guidelines are intended to explain and serve as a resource for the con-ferral of the *mandatum*.

Our Hearts Were Burning Within Us (1999). See Part Four for a discussion of this pastoral plan for adult education.

Other Publications

Alice Gallin, OSU. *Independence and a New Partnership in Catholic Higher Education.* Notre Dame, IN: University of Notre Dame Press, 1996. A narrative and analysis of a major shift in the governance of Catholic colleges and universities—from religious orders to laity.

Francis Oakley and Bruce Russett, eds. *Governance, Accountability and the Future of the Catholic Church.* New York: Continuum International Publishing Group, 2004. This book grew out of the 2002 conference at Yale described in Part Four. Contributors include church historians Francine Cardman and Gerald Fogarty, SJ; canonist Father John Beal; journalist and former *Commonweal* editor Peter Steinfels; Bishop Donald Wuerl of Pittsburgh; Francis J. Butler, president of FADICA (Founders and Donors Interested in Catholic Activities); and many others.

Report of the Church in America, Leadership Roundtable 2004. Contains the substance of panel discussions on a variety of topics relevant to church accountability and management practices with recommendations for change. The conference on which this report is based is briefly discussed in Part Four. The report is available from the Leadership Roundtable located in the FADICA office.

INDEX

Ad Gentes, xi
Adult education, 25, 95
America magazine, 73
Anderson, Paul, 55
Apostolicam Actuositatem, xi, xiii, 2,
        13, 15, 16, 17, 21, 22, 24,
        26, 27, 29, 30, 32, 37, 56,
        57, 63, 66, 67, 77, 78, 82,
        86, 87, 88, 95

Baptism, 3, 17, 19, 21
Bellisolo, Pilar, 12
Benedict, St., 4
Benedictines, 90
Bernardin, Joseph, 47, 62, 65, 68,
        93
Bevilacqua, Anthony, 64
Bishops' Committee on the Laity
        (NCCB), 39, 55, 80
Blatt, Genevieve, 42
Boston College, 94
Butler, Francis, 46
Byrne, Leo, 68

Call to Action (1974–1976), 41–47,
        49, 51
"Call to Action" lay organization,
        50
Called and Gifted, 55–61, 63–64, 83
Cardign, Joseph, 4–5, 8–9
Castel Gandolfo, 12

Casti Connubii, 22
Catechism of the Catholic Church, 92
Catholic Action, 4–5, 8, 18, 32–33
Catholic schools, 24–25
Catholic social thought, 4
Catholic University of America,
        The, 10, 46
Catholic Worker Movement, 4
Catholics United for the Faith
        (CUF), 53
Cento, Fernando, 17
Charisms, 27
Chesterton, G. K., 7
Chittister, Joan, OSB, 72
Christian Family Movement
        (CFM), 4, 11
Christian Life Communities, 53
Christifideles Laici, 19, 59, 61, 66–67
Church in America; Leadership
        Roundtable, 87
Church of the 21st Century, 94
Clark, Matthew, 72–73
Clarke, Thomas, SJ, 14
Clericalism, 17
Cody, John, 43
Cold war, 4
Common Ground Award (2005), 95
Communion and Liberation, 65
Community, 58, 66, 79
Confraternity of Christian
        Doctrine (CCD), 11

Congar, Yves, OP, 2–3, 9
Congregation for the Doctrine of
the Faith, 67
Consulting the laity, 62–64
Co-workers in the Vineyard of the
Lord, 89–90
Cursillo Movement, 28, 78

Day, Dorothy, 4, 15
Deardon, John, 38–39, 41, 45, 49
De Roo, Remy, 17, 21
Dialogue, 24, 80
Diekman, Godfrey, OSB, 14
Dignatatis Humanae, 16, 23–24, 41
Doepfner, Julius, 16
Domestic church, 30
D'Souza, Eugene, 18
Dulles, Avery, 90
Dunne, John, 73–74
Duquesne University, 72
Duval, Léon-Etienne, 20

Eastern rite, 20
Ecclesiam Suam, 52, 88
Ecumenical Institute of
Spirituality, 14
Ecumenism, 81
Engaged Encounter, 78
Equal Rights Amendment (ERA),
68, 69
Evangelization, 30
Evans, George, 55
Ex Corde Ecclesiae, 82, 84

Family Rosary, 15
Feminism, 74–75
Filteau, Jerry, 45
First World Congress for the Lay
Apostolate, 6–7
Focolare, 65
Follow the Way of Love, 75

Foyer Unitas, 15
Francis of Assisi, St., 51
Frings, Joseph, 16
From Words to Deeds, 74
Frye, Mariella, MHSH, 71–72

Gallin, Alice, OSU, 43, 81
Gaudium et Spes, 2, 13, 23, 26, 27,
49, 66
Gerety, Peter Leo, 43, 44, 48, 49
Gleason, Philip, 42
Globalization, 29
Goldie, Rosemary, 5, 7, 8, 9, 12, 38
Governance, 19
Grace, Margie, 15
Gracias, Valerian, 7
Grady, Thomas, 55, 68
Grail, The, 4–6
Gravissimum Educationis, 22, 23, 57,
66, 81–83, 92, 95
Greek Orthodox, 14
Guiton, Jean, 12

Heenan, John, 21
Hoffman, James, 55, 90
Holiness, 57
Holy Year 1950, 6
Hughes, Jean Wolford, 45
Human Life in Our Time, 84

Ignatius of Antioch, St., 18
Imesch, Joseph, 71
Individuals in the apostolate, 31
Informal networks, 31
Instruction on Certain Questions
Regarding the Collaboration
of the Non-Ordained Faith-
ful in the Sacramental
Ministry of Priests, 89
International Catholic Workers'
Movement, 12

Jones, Patricia, 65
John XXIII, Pope, 1, 3, 14
John Paul I, Pope, 51
John Paul II, Pope, 38, 51, 67, 69, 75

Keegan, Patrick, 12
Kelly, Thomas, OP, 47, 48
Krol, John, 16, 60

La Cugna, Catherine Mowry, 76
L'Arche Movement, 65
Ladies of Bethany, 15
Laity
    as church representatives, 18
    collaboration of, 25, 32, 34
    consultation of, 62–64
    spiritual formation of, 35
    theological education of, 35
    vocation of, 26
Lakeland, Paul, 2
Lay apostolate, 5, 6
    objectives of the, 28–29
Lay auditors, 11
Lay ecclesial ministry, 77, 86, 89, 91
Lay ministry, 24, 51, 64–65, 90
Leadership, 91
    in education, 84–85, 93
LeClerc, Jean, OSB, 14
Legion of Mary, 15, 19
Leven, Stephen, 19
Lonergan, Bernard, SJ, 4, 36
Lubich, Chiara, 65
Lucker, Raymond, 55
Lumen Gentium, 2, 12, 17–19, 27, 35, 49, 57–58

Mahony, Roger, 64–65
Mandatum, 82
Marriage, 22, 23, 26, 30, 66, 77–78
Marriage Encounter, 28

May, John, 62, 66
McAuliffe, Michael, 67–70
McCarthy, Edward, 50, 52–54
Meaney, George, 9
Meyer, Albert, 16
Ministry, 30, 57, 60
Montessori, Maria, 11
Mulieres Dignitatem, 67
Murphy, P. Francis, 68
Murray, John Courtney, SJ, 41–42
Muslims, 20
Muto, Susan, 72

National Advisory Council (NAC), 39–41, 49, 54, 55
National Catholic Education Association, 10
National Council of Catholic Laity (NCCL), 53, 54
National Council of Catholic Men, 53
National Council of Catholic Women, 53, 70
Newman, John Henry, 7
Nobel Peace Prize, 79
Non-Christian religions, document on, 16
Noonan, John, 68
North American Conference of Separated and Divorced Catholics, 53, 79

Oblates, 90
O'Brien, David, 42, 48
Opus Dei, 78
Orsy, Ladislas, SJ, 88
Ordinatio Sacerdotalis, 73
Ott, Stanley, 62
Ottenweller, Albert, 53, 60–61
Our Hearts Were Burning Within Us, 95

Parish life, 64
Patriarchal ideology, 75
Paul VI, Pope, 9, 11–12, 16, 22, 38,
    42, 46, 51–52, 88
Pax Romana, 5–6
Pius X, Pope, 1
Pius XII, Pope, 1, 6, 8
Pontifical Council for the Family,
    38
Pontifical Council on the Laity, 2,
    38, 67

Quinn, John, 69

Rahner, Karl, SJ, 9
Rausch, James, 46
Religious education, 23
Renewing the Vision: Sons and
    Daughters of the Light, 95
Ritter, Joseph, 16, 17, 19
Roach, John, 69, 71
Roe v. Wade, 68
Roman Catholic/Presbyterian,
    Reformed Consultation, 80
Rosazza, Peter, 55
Rynne, Xavier, 17

St. Joan's Alliance, 74
San Egidio Community, 79
Schaeffer, Catherine, 7
Schillebeeckx, Edward, 9
Schneiders, Sandra, IHM, 74–75
School of Sacred Theology (Saint
    Mary's College, Notre
    Dame, Indiana), 10, 25
Second World Congress (for the
    Lay Apostolate), 8, 19
Secretariat for the Laity (within the
    Curia), 21, 37
Secretariat for the Laity (NCCB),
    50

Seper, Franjo, 20
Seton, Elizabeth Ann, 42
Sex abuse scandals, 62, 86–87, 93
Sex education, 23, 84
Sexism, 72
Sheed, Frank, 7
Sheed & Ward Publishing Com-
    pany, 7, 42
Sheehan, Michael, 47–48
Sister Formation Movement, 10
Sisters of Mercy of the Americas,
    90
Snyder, John, 70, 73
Social justice education, 93
Society of Jesus, 91
Solidarity, 31
Sorbonne, 5–6
Spirituality, 27–28, 64, 77, 87, 91
Steere, Douglas, 14
Stewardship, 87
Strengthening the Bonds of Peace,
    73–74
Suenens, Leon-Joseph, 15–16, 18,
    27
Suhard, Emmanuel, 7
Sullivan, John, 69–70
Sydney University, 6
Synod on Catechetics, 71
Synod on Marriage and Family,
    38
Synod on Vocation and Mission of
    the Laity in the Church
    and in the World, 5,
    18–19, 61–62, 64

Teaching, as vocation, 24
Teens Encounter Christ, 78
Templeton Award, 65
Thérèse of Lisieux, St., 4
Thomas Aquinas, St., 2
To Teach as Jesus Did, 83–84, 92

Trappists, 91
Trisco, Robert, 42
Tromp, Sebastian, SJ, 8

Unitatis Redintegratio, 35
United Nations, 7

Vanier, Jean, 65
Van Kamm, Adrian, 72
Voice of the Faithful, 88

Ward, Barbara, 13, 65
Ward, Maisie, 7
Weakland, Rembert, OSB, 62
Women, 4, 10, 12, 13, 18, 29, 38,
        60, 64, 67, 74, 91
Women, pastoral letter on, 67

Women and the diaconate, 70
Women's Ordination Conference
        (WOC), 69–71
Work, Martin, 15
World Baptist Alliance, 14
World Union of Catholic Women's
        Organizations, 12
World Youth Day, xiii

Yale University, 94
Young Christian Students (YCS),
        4, 8
Young Christian Workers (YCW), 4
Youth, xiii, 30, 38
Yugoslavia, 31

Zoghby, Elias, 20